Human Renaissance

The New World of Your Power

CLARE FINLEY McCORD, Ph.D.

New Renaissance Press
Miami Beach, Florida

New Renaissance Press
1521 Alton Road, Suite 232
Miami Beach, Florida 33139

www.humanrenaissance.com

Neither the author nor the publisher is engaged in offering professional medical or health advice to readers. The recommendations, suggestions and techniques contained in this book are intended to provide general information. They are not a substitute for consulting with your physician or other healthcare provider. You should seek medical advice and supervision for all matters regarding your health. Neither the author nor the publisher shall be responsible for any harm, loss or damage arising from any recommendation, suggestion, technique or other content in this book.

Book design by Thomas White, Imprint Media

ISBN: 978-0-9908424-0-8

To my family, friends, and teachers—in this and other dimensions,
And to you
With love and gratitude.

Contents

Part Three
Challenges to Power

Foreword

Clare McCord has written a delicious book that challenges us to step in with consciousness to participate in a Renaissance that is actually going on in all of us. She shares a wealth of information she has gathered over thirty years of study and practice. I know how seriously and passionately Clare embraces the work of personal power and health, and how deeply committed she is to helping others learn and use new tools.

Since she is a teacher, Clare is able to take complex or difficult concepts and make them easy to understand. Her own experiences and adventures make the ideas and techniques memorable. This book speaks to us on so many levels about our own very real power, the power that we have by being just ourselves.

Clare's perspective is unique because she has spent so much of her life studying, experiencing, and practicing alternative health and healing while pursuing demanding careers in the academic and corporate worlds. The book reflects her rare ability to understand, connect, and apply what she has learned from the often disconnected worlds that we live in every day. Her journey to new worlds happens while she participates in the real world of work and life, and that's her point – we can all experience and create an expanded, healthier life.

Human Renaissance delivers a convincing and serious message about the need for all of us to expand our awareness and use our innate talents, but Clare makes it personal and even fun. And the best part is, she tells you how to do it. I love this book. I recommend it highly.

Donna Eden
Author of *Energy Medicine* and *The Energies of Love*

Special Thank-You to My Dad

As a special preface to this work, I want to thank my father, Jim McCord, for showing me the powerful ways our beliefs create reality—for better or for worse; for his amazing intellect, which never faded; for his extreme integrity; for his belief in the dignity of everyday people; for his contagious sense of humor; and, finally, for his ability, in his last years, to open himself to the possibility of a new world.

In the last week of my dad's life, he was hospitalized. It took me a couple of days to get arrangements made to travel to him, knowing that this was probably his final week. During the two days I prepared to go, we talked by phone between his meals and medical procedures. Although I had just spoken to him at noon the day before I left, about 4:00 he had a nurse phone and ask me to please call him. Dad was very frugal; actually, he was cheap. The hospital phone is free for incoming calls. So I knew he must still be pretty much alive!

Remembering our conversation still gives me goose bumps. I share it because of its relevance to human renaissance principles; it is such a fabulous demonstration of our natural human abilities.

Here's what he wanted to talk about. He opened the conversation by saying that I was the only person he knew who would understand what he was experiencing based on the alternative study I had done over the years. "You'll be able to help me, Clarey," he said, "because you know about all this oddball stuff." He added, "Maybe you can tell me if I'm hallucinating."

He went on to describe an altered state of consciousness that he had been experiencing most of the day. Many readers will relate to Dad's experience if they have been present during the dying process of a friend or loved one, as the consciousness opens and expands, preparing one to leave the limitations of the physical world.

During our hour-long conversation, Dad described seeing things that were "just not logical." The highlights were:

- He could "see through" people when they came in to speak with him. Nurses, doctors, or other professionals looked like what he called "webs" that were completely transparent, but had a sort of substance.
- He found that he had multiple spatial perspectives, although not intentionally. For example, the floor, walls, and ceiling would trade places, so he felt he was zooming about the landscape of the room, not maintaining the "correct" spatial orientation. This made him dizzy, of course. It came and went, as did the other phenomena.
- He could "see through the ceiling as if it's not there." When I asked him what he saw instead, he described lots of shapes: paramecia, fluid ovals, figure eights, geometric shapes, and lines that looked like equations without numbers (Dad was an engineer and a mathematics genius).
- Finally, he said softly, "There are people who have been coming in that I know cannot be here." I asked if some were from the past or other parts of his life, and he said yes. I asked if Mom and other relatives had been there, and he said yes.

We had a long and surprisingly matter-of-fact discussion about the world of energy, frequency, consciousness, and generally about the invisible aspects of our world. He had read Donna Eden's book *Energy Medicine* (1998), and he knew she saw people's energy. He quipped, "Maybe I can see that stuff, too." I was very proud of him. Of course, the next sentence was, "Well, but I may be hallucinating since this is so illogical. The doctors tell me that the medicine may make it worse." Nevertheless, he had called, and he had reached out. Most importantly, he believed in me and respected my knowledge of that alien alternative world in which I had spent so many years.

We ended the call by agreeing that the best course of action was for him to try to accept his altered state and even enjoy it if he could, understanding that he might just be glimpsing aspects of reality usually inaccessible to us. He laughed when I suggested that some people paid large sums of money and even broke the law for experiences like his. We did not discuss his death directly, but I think we both knew that this was a crucial step toward his final transition, and we had taken it together.

My dad gave me a magnificent gift that day. A very private man, he could have kept his experience to himself, but he chose to reach out. This event made me even more determined to complete my book and commit to help as many people as possible experience and enjoy a new, expanded, more powerful life.

On Using This Book

Use of Language in This Book

Language – no matter which one – carries intention and the power to change reality. In this book, I often use language in non-traditional ways to provoke new thought. Language is one of our most powerful tools and one that many of us take for granted. The mastery of this tool, for communicators and language "consumers," pays huge dividends. I am reminded of the statement often attributed to Winston Churchill regarding the difference between the British and Americans: "We are two people separated by a common language." This perceptive remark highlights a principle of our almost limitless diversity: we can create entirely different realities for different audiences, using the same words and phrases.

Throughout the book, I often call attention to language by using a hyphenated spelling of certain words such as "re-view," "co-incidence," or "dis-ease" to shift focus to a more literal meaning of those words in keeping with the book's key principle of heightened awareness and seeing things in new ways. I encourage readers to take a new look at all words for their possible expanded meanings—especially the very literal ones that we usually miss!

Special Terms

Instead of a glossary of terms, I define jargon or special terms either in the text when I use them or in an endnote. For further reference, I recommend Linnie Thomas' *The Encyclopedia of Energy Medicine* (2010) and the comprehensive descriptions in Nenah Sylver's *The Rife Handbook of Frequency Therapy with a Holistic Health Primer* (2009).

Below, I define a few alternative health terms to provide some foundation.

Modality – This term is often used in the alternative health field to denote any one specific type of healthcare approach or system. The word has gained popularity and meaning as more options have appeared. I use it to mean a health approach or system of any genre.

Allopathic medicine – I use this term to denote what we think of as "mainstream medicine," the diagnostic/intervention and specialty-based healthcare model that most people use. Sometimes we call this "western medicine," to distinguish it from "eastern medicine" systems such as traditional Chinese medicine or Ayurveda. It is also sometimes called "modern medicine."

Alternative medicine – This term denotes any healthcare modality that is not considered allopathic medicine. Alternative approaches are often called "complementary" to describe their relationship to allopathic medicine. In addition to eastern medicine systems, this includes such modalities as osteopathy, homeopathy, naturopathy, anthroposophical medicine, and many more. All holistic approaches – literally those that consider the whole person – also fall under this category.

Key Messages

Throughout the book, I highlight key messages by bolding them and placing them within two horizontal lines so that they will stand out. The messages provide special insights and summarize content from the sections in which they appear. They deliver key points in a memorable way, and can help you locate and review material that you find particularly interesting or useful.

Materials Just for You

Throughout the book I present suggestions, techniques, and exercises that I have developed and used successfully. Exercises or techniques are set off graphically so they can be easily located and used. Readers can find more materials and resources on the Human Renaissance website. Just go to www.humanrenaissance.com. Feel free to contact me to discuss other ways Human Renaissance®

educational products may be of service to you or your organization. For organizational coaching or consulting, please also visit www.mccordconsulting.com. I hope you will use this book as part of your life and your own renaissance.

Preface

For more than three decades, I have explored the alternative realms of what we have come to call the New Age. My journey began because of a serious health issue, but as I learned how to be healthy, I wanted to know more. It became my passion to study, experience, and practice alternative philosophies and health modalities. What I learned and experienced forms the basis for this book.

In a nutshell, *I learned that we are powerful beings who are not taught to use the many aspects of our innate wisdom and power.* In fact, most of us are trained to think and act in ways that directly oppose our natural, healthy resources. I became aware also of the many influences that serve to keep our power limited or unavailable to us. As I learned more about this, I knew I had to write this book.

My studies also taught me that *accessing our power means learning to harness invisible forces*, such as mental and emotional power, the energy of consciousness, and the limitless unseen world of energy around and within us. These resources, however, have been either flatly denied by conventional culture or used in very restricted ways. Certainly, nothing about these frontiers of human power had been taught in my extensive conventional education.

Human power is a precious commodity, so knowledge of its key precepts was kept safely in mystery schools and secret societies for centuries. Even in the late twentieth century, despite an overwhelming array of self-help materials, I found it was startlingly difficult and costly to learn more about my own human assets. To make matters worse, instant Internet access combined with a burgeoning alternative industry created an overabundance of resources with no reliable best-practice "filters." How could I tell the credible teachers or healers from the New Age opportunists or just plain weirdos? Truth was, I often couldn't, and had to use trial and error until I developed enough knowledge to make good choices.

I am still astounded at the lack of good information available to us regarding valid research on alternative health techniques. In fact, there is a huge body of literature and much great research, but this information is not easily accessible. Compounding this challenge, many alternative health systems function as discrete modalities, so access to the big picture of the field is a difficult task. There are lots of systems and approaches, but few people connecting the dots for the public.

Not everyone can or should have to take the long and expensive journey I have taken, nor should they have to work so hard to locate common threads among the many alternative modalities and philosophies. I have no healing method to sell, just a desire to bring the common threads together and to help people have a stronger foundation to make good health and life decisions based on information that is more comprehensive.

With this in mind, I began making notes for a book that could be a regular person's guide to the vast array of tools available to help discover and use our human capabilities. To create real change, the information needed to touch real people, not just those who could visit gurus or afford the high cost of seminars in resort areas. The phrase "human renaissance" kept coming to me in dreams and when I would doodle. Having been a student and teacher of Renaissance English literature, I could see the Renaissance parallels in our current situation.

I intend my work to be more provocative than prescriptive. I do not offer my experience as professional or medical advice. I see myself as an explorer, a facilitator, and an educator. Throughout my own journey, I have used my body/mind as a living laboratory within what I consider to be safe parameters. In *Human Renaissance,* I offer perspectives and describe my experiences to motivate new thinking about key issues, as well as to encourage individuals and organizations to begin actively working toward new models of education for all people.

This book can be a bridge to help transport us from ideas and techniques we think of as New Age to much wider applications that can move us into a very real—and much needed—New World. By discovering, valuing, and using our immense suite of human abilities and by cooperating to educate as many people as possible, we can create our new world. In that spirit, I offer *Human Renaissance* to you. Thank you for taking the time to read and re-view.

Part One
Our Renaissance

1
THE HUMAN RENAISSANCE

From Columbus to Copernicus, from Copernicus to Galileo, from the discovery of earth to that of the heavens . . . Man refound himself.

Jules Michelet, *Renaissance* (1855)

A renaissance of human consciousness and creation is underway which will far surpass the discoveries of the legendary historical era. Renaissance literally means "rebirth." Global, collective, and individual crises have acted as catalysts for a rebirth of ourselves. In the words of French historian Jules Michelet, the time has come once again for us to "refind" ourselves.[1]

In the first renaissance, we rediscovered lost wisdom and culture, and discovered previously unknown aspects of our physical world – our earth, our bodies, the solar system and galaxy around us. Our human renaissance now takes us to vaster and more subtle new worlds as we rediscover the lost wisdom of our own being, and learn to understand and harness a universe of previously invisible power.

We have all become explorers. Every person I know is undergoing significant life changes right now. More and more people have reached a point where they are looking for their own new world – a re-creation, a renaissance of all aspects of life. We find ourselves having to navigate our way into a *new world*, because the *old world* no longer supports us.

Few people on this planet feel exempt from the shifts happening at all levels: physical, economic, emotional, mental, collective, and individual. Almost every structure we have created to organize and operate our world seems to be failing, whether it be business, economics, healthcare, education, or even religion. The earth itself is under stress, and threats to our environment are now a clear and present danger. Wars continue to proliferate, and the constant threat of large-scale nuclear destruction remains. All this creates a continuous level of tension that affects all daily life, made worse by the continuous media barrage. This high stress level causes extreme discomfort, which also acts as a catalyst for a renaissance of positive change.

Three key trends signal the emergence of a human renaissance and echo cultural phenomena that have roots in the historical Renaissance. These are:

- **The individual and collective readiness to discover previously unknown new worlds**. In the Renaissance, a wave of discovery in all areas of human endeavor formed the foundation for much of our modern knowledge. Until they are discovered, new worlds remain unknown. But they are there, awaiting discovery, like North America, microbes, or the atom. Today, our discoveries increasingly focus on phenomena that are there, but invisible – electromagnetic frequency, quantum physics, new uses for light and sound. The readiness to explore these invisible worlds is key to our current renaissance.
- **A new recognition of the abilities and value of real people**. In the Renaissance, middle class people became educated and entered areas of society previously closed to anyone but nobility and clergy. Today, through social media and other web-based vehicles such as YouTube and blogs, the thoughts and activities of everyday people have become almost too available. Television programming markets to this trend as well, with a variety of reality shows that have also grown in number and popularity. Although (and because) this trend has been commercialized, it represents an important indicator of our collective belief in the value of each person's talents and abilities.
- **Greater opportunity for more people to engage in the process of change through advances in technology.**

> The Renaissance invention and use of the printing press resulted in the first information technology quantum leap. New knowledge could be shared with a greater audience due to increased literacy and a world that was more connected by increased international travel. Today's renaissance relies upon one of the greatest technology leaps in history—the Internet. Now, an immense population makes use of expanded media and communication to form a global engine for discovery and creation.

I believe that our renaissance is now at an exciting "tipping point" where we can all benefit from these trends as we expand our abilities to discover, share, and use resources that have been invisible to most of us.

DISCOVERING UNKNOWN WORLDS

> *Man cannot discover new oceans unless he has the courage to lose sight of the shore.*
>
> Andre Gide

On their voyages of discovery, Renaissance explorers saw the horizon as the limit of the visible world. These explorers left the shores of their known world to navigate in unknown waters, moving beyond the horizon into a previously invisible world. In order to discover a new world, they had to trust that it existed. These brave souls *challenged previously defined limits to expand everyone's ability to see what was already there.*

Our current renaissance calls us again to challenge our limits, to question our ideas and definitions of the possible or the real. Once again, we will expand our vision to find a new world waiting for us – already there. The key to successful discovery now lies in developing the power to see, understand and use innate and natural resources that have been previously hidden, or even forbidden.

This renaissance focuses on real people and on practical uses for many skills and abilities that have been characterized as extra-ordinary or para-normal, when they are really just part of being human. Real people can access an expanded toolkit by re-learning things about ourselves that have gone unrecognized for generations. We learn first to see and then to use previously invisible human capabilities. In turn, using our new tools helps us to discover previously invisible opportunities and create previously impossible results.

An experience years ago helped me to understand and process the immense power of seeing things in new ways. I often call attention to this by hyphenation of the word "re-view." During a tour I took of the Grand Canyon, a park ranger explained to our group how the human mind comprehends the enormity of the canyon. He said, "Because we have no known reference for seeing anything this huge up close, for seeing a canyon so enormous it can hold a mountain, our brains literally re-format the scene, so it is manageable. Just like when you rent a movie and the message pops up, THIS HAS BEEN RE-FORMATTED TO FIT YOUR SCREEN."

Three important points arise from this wonderful analogy:

1. The mind re-formats all data to fit the *existing screen* of the observer.
2. When faced with something unknown, radically new, or different, the mind will find concepts, images, and proportions that are comfortable, so that seeing, perceiving, or understanding is possible.
3. The inability to locate a familiar construct to make sense of new data may cause us to "see" nothing at all!

My favorite example of this dilemma of sight is the story about the first Native Americans to encounter Columbus' huge, alien ships. As the story goes, these people, who had nothing like those sailing ships in their mental database, could see that the ocean waters were disturbed, but saw no ships. After a shaman spent days gazing at the disturbed water asking for new wisdom to see, he finally saw the invaders. But by then, they were too close to shore for the people to flee or defend. The ships existed, but the native people's minds had no analog to process the image until it became a dangerously real experience.

The metaphor of learning to see the ships permeates this work and informs the human renaissance. Throughout the book, we will look at the various ways our vision—of physical and conceptual phenomena—may be disabled or blocked, and how we can open ourselves to new possibilities. The key components of the new world may be right under our noses, but we cannot discover them unless we are willing to (in the words of *Star Trek*) "boldly go" into invisible frontiers, "where no man has gone before."

Star Trek and other science fiction stories call attention to the importance of moving beyond our known world. They also provide many clues to tools and abilities we can develop. People often remark how many futuristic devices and capabilities formerly in the province of science fiction are now well-accepted features of everyday life. As it often does, fiction provides us with a pre-view of future realities.

The *Star Trek* prologue asserted that space was the "final frontier." *We* are the new final frontier, with all our unexplored capabilities and power.

The more we open to explore, discover, and expand, the greater our renaissance. We can take the teachings from what we have called the New Age and apply them to realize a New World.

Renaissance Echoes

Our current renaissance echoes many of the themes of the historical period and builds on its foundations. A brief re-view of the period illustrates themes and lessons we can use as we navigate our journey. As you read this section, you may make your own connections to current trends or events.

Much like today, in the Renaissance an increasingly curious, financially able, and educated public combined with a more connected world to foster a wave of great discovery. Similar to our challenges today, a massive creative tension produced new ideas and new approaches to all areas of human endeavor. The atmosphere was one of anxiety and excitement. Political unrest, wars, and dis-ease played counterpoint to the bold beauty of new art, music, literature and the wonders of new science, medicine and exotic civilizations.

Renaissance discoveries of new worlds in so many areas caused dramatic perceptual shifts that we now accept as part of our known world. All of these discoveries, as we know, represented expanded ability to see what was already part of the existing world.

In a renaissance, the previously unthinkable and invisible become real.

Renaissance painters' depiction of enhanced dimensional perspective gave viewers new vision, as the two-dimensional figures of the mediaeval times gave way to three-dimensional and experimental work of the fourteenth through seventeenth centuries. In the fields of medicine and anatomy, cadavers were studied to discover the previously invisible frontier of our own bodies. A spirit of exploration and experimentation drove pursuits in all realms: theater, music, art, medicine, science, literature, philosophy, and even religion.

To find their way into new worlds, Renaissance writers, artists, scientists, and philosophers often returned to the wisdom of the ancient world – Greeks, Romans, Hebrews, Egyptians, and others, to learn their secrets. A return to ancient texts provided insight into long-lost ways of seeing, being, and creating. Renaissance scholars, authors, and professionals also leapt into realms of esoteric and supernatural phenomena. The revival of ancient mystery texts and their wisdom provided keys to re-discovery of old knowledge, and the old world became new again.

People revived as much ancient knowledge as possible and gave it new life. This included religious, spiritual, philosophical, and esoteric texts, as well as treatises on sacred geometry, numerology, and even frequency. Our own New Age explorers have taken similar journeys to knowledge which was already there, but which had been forgotten or intentionally withheld from people in order to control them.

Then, as now, renaissance discoveries often challenged the status quo—especially if those discoveries could not be controlled for power or profit. One good example is that those who explored what we might consider alternative healthcare, like the ancient folkways of herbal or energetic healing, were often persecuted as witches or magicians. Anyone who publicly presented or applied challenging doctrines, whether they were healers, philosophers, poets, politicians, or scientists, could be subject to censure or worse by those whose power depended on maintaining things "as they have always been."

During the Middle Ages and Renaissance, the power elite

controlled the masses through a strict economic hierarchy and local control delivered primarily via cultural/religious means. For the regular person living during the Renaissance, being human was far from an asset. People often lived in a state of lifelong spiritual, mental, emotional, and physical condemnation just because they were human. Beliefs based on original sin created a consciousness blockade against individual or collective belief in human power—equating being human with being permanently limited and fatally flawed. This deep self-limiting belief persists, appearing in our everyday language in such phrases as "to err is human," or "I am only human."

Until the Renaissance, only members of the ruling elite received education and were literate, so only they had access to the types of learning we might call symbolic or abstract, and only they had opportunity to explore human boundaries—physical, mental, emotional, or spiritual—without penalty. The majority of the people, however, lived without opportunity to develop expanded awareness. For them, there was no formal education, and there usually was no escape from a life cycle of work, disease, and death.

In addition to teachings that stressed human limitation and suffering, public displays of torture and death acted as an intense type of early media campaign to deter people from too much exploration or discovery. In these displays, punishments such as evisceration (think about the final scenes of the 1995 movie *Braveheart*) were designed to highlight the human body as a vehicle of fear and pain. In the ages before the rank and file could read, this served as effective media manipulation and control.

People's vivid memories of public torture and punishment were effectively employed as tools to force people to confess to witchcraft and other crimes. This practice, called *territio verbalis* (Latin for verbal terror) involved forcing the prisoner to listen to lengthy and graphic descriptions of the torture they could expect to undergo if they did not confess. These extremely effective fear tactics often lasted for days. Even after having confessed, the prisoner was most often tortured anyway for the public effect.

The famous and well-respected Renaissance astronomer, mathematician, and philosopher, Johannes Kepler, had to use all his skill and influence to save his own mother from such charges and practices over a difficult period lasting from 1617 to 1621, during which she was accused, imprisoned, and tried for witchcraft. Ironically, at this time, Kepler was also completing one of his best known works, *Harmonices Mundi* (1619), which explained the harmonics of the world cosmos based on the mathematical "music of the spheres" first set forth by Pythagoras and others. Kepler succeeded in freeing his mother, but most accused "witches" did not have such an accomplished and well-connected advocate.

Renaissance scientists often fared worse than witches, as they risked not only imprisonment, torture and cruel death, but also the banning or censure of their life's work. Three famous examples were Nicolaus Copernicus, Giordano Bruno, and Galileo Galilei. Astronomer Nicolaus Copernicus (1473-1543) beat the system. He published his treatise *De Revolutionibus Orbium Celestium* (*Of the Revolution of the Celestial Spheres*) on his deathbed to make sure he was unavailable for punishment. Building on Copernicus' theories, Giordano Bruno (1548-1600) espoused an infinite universe that included not only one sun and solar system, but many. Bruno was a prolific author and lecturer, and ultimately his views cost him his life. He was tried and imprisoned for seven years under the Inquisition, and finally burned at the stake in Rome in 1600.

Often considered the father of modern experimental science, Galileo (1564-1642) also built on Copernicus' solar system model. Galileo was interrogated for almost a year under the Inquisition. Kept under arrest and threatened with torture, he was also banned from publishing his work describing the planetary system that today we take as a given. Luckily, he was well-enough connected that he continued to write and publish until the end of his life, although he died in ill-health and under extreme stress.

Although scientists who venture outside current norms in today's culture are usually not imprisoned or tortured, they nevertheless risk ridicule, loss of funding, and censure by *status quo* organizations. Orthopedic surgeon and researcher Robert Becker draws directly on Renaissance history when describing his experience being "grilled" by a research committee unlikely to accept his new ideas about using electrical current for bone and limb regeneration. After hearing his project called "unscientific," "charlatanistic," and worse, Becker recalls that "I had the momentary thrill of imagining myself as Galileo or Giordano Bruno; I thought of walking to the window to see if the stake and faggots were set up on the lawn."[2] Explorers still risk safety to discover new worlds.

Safety for any person in the historical Renaissance was far from guaranteed. Conditions set up many of the beliefs about being human that we carry within us to this day. Since Renaissance life offered regular people few rewards and many possible punishments, people learned that if they obeyed the rules, life's painful struggle could have a payoff: a much-hoped-for trip to heaven after death. Once freed from "human bondage," one could soar. Human life was not seen as having a high value; instead it was viewed as a long struggle necessary to achieve the goal of becoming pure spirit.

This was understandable, since Renaissance life was often difficult and short because of poor overall sanitation, a lack of healthcare, and rampant disease. Even privileged and noble people had short life expectancies, leading to the popularity of *carpe diem* (Latin for "seize the day") themes in art, music, and poetry. Pressure was intense for professionals or artists to have prolific careers when they were quite young.

Unchecked mass disease was a major cause of death. Plagues ravaged Europe and England in unpredictable waves. People who could not afford to escape metropolitan areas were subject to the full impact of the Grim Reaper, while those who could afford to flee escaped to rural homes to wait out the outbreaks, which often followed them anyway. There were no guarantees and no medical treatment options for most people. Today, even without the Renaissance plagues, the lack of health care and daily risk sounds much too familiar, especially in urban populations. The result is a pervasive cultural pressure that often produces creative greatness, especially in the young.

We are once again seeing a trend toward precocious young professionals becoming successful in our culture. Today's pressure on the young is different from that of the Renaissance, but it is no less intense. One good example would be the growing number of really young performers on shows like *The Voice*, *American Idol,* or the *X-Factor.* Children are maturing faster, assisted by daily media access, and they are showing up in the media more and more. The pressure to get out there and be seen – to make a statement in public

– has become part of life for the young, who become minor celebs every day, using a variety of personal and social media. Advanced technologies afford almost everyone a stage, a platform to be famous.

The creative pressures of the Renaissance resulted in an economic, educational, and expressive liberation of a new class of people, the middle class. This rising group created invisible waves of excitement and innovation that permeated all areas of endeavor. The energy of this ambitious class shifted the consciousness of all people on the planet. Even without the Internet, it "went viral." The flowering and abundance of this invisible movement became visible in creations everywhere—art, music, education, writing, medicine, exploration, and business.

The Renaissance saw the dawn of economic opportunity and upward mobility for regular people. For the first time in history, global business was not owned solely by the Crown, the Church, and a few ruling families. The entrance of the new middle class into the world of business forever altered values in the civilized world by re-defining social status and opportunity in economic terms. Middle class people had broken through a crucial barrier. They acquired economic power that freed them from the web of basic survival issues, allowing them to move into a new world, a new way of life.

Whereas previously only nobility were educated, universities began to admit non-noble students because they could afford to pay for the privilege. This revolutionary development added a new phrase to the English language that we still use today. When a non-noble student was enrolled, his status was noted by his name with the Latin phrase *sine nobilitatis,* meaning "without nobility" and abbreviated "s.nob." Thus, our word "snob" was born.

Queen Elizabeth I of England (1558–1603), one of the most famous female leaders in history, stands as a major icon of the Renaissance.[3] She was also possibly the first self-created media star, a role model for any number of today's celebrities. In addition to financing voyages of discovery (and of course military conquests) and acting as a patron of the arts and sciences, Elizabeth was unique and innovative in her use of political, rhetorical, and "media" tactics to gain and maintain her throne through many decades.

Carefully crafting a public image of herself as the Virgin Queen, Elizabeth never married, deftly managed her public and private suitors, and used all available public media to show herself as a goddess-like figure. All of her actions strengthened her ability to rule as a woman in a man's world, no easy task. Her many public "progresses" were lavish and costly road shows, media campaigns to impress the rank and file as well as the nobility. The campaigns used larger-than-life symbols—costumes and props evoking classical myths—to elevate Elizabeth to the status of a goddess, usually Athena, and thus to implant the images of her rule as divine.

With a few alterations for modern audiences, Elizabeth's media playbook could still be quite successful. In fact, a look at the way almost any modern female celebrity crafts her public persona would no doubt reveal parallels to Elizabeth's many tactics. The Renaissance provided foundations not just in the creation and use of a secular public media, but in all areas of business and culture. The extreme re-creations in the arts, sciences, business, economics, and daily life provided the building blocks of our modern world.

Today we have reached a new plateau. In our current renaissance, we are again drawn to invisible frontiers—outside and within ourselves. Now, we not only accept the invisible world, our lives revolve around it. Our society has become dependent upon an entire constellation of devices that access invisible phenomena—wireless everything: cell phones, smart phones, the web itself. And there can be no doubt that opportunity for great numbers of regular people has grown exponentially as the invisible "web" opens vast frontiers, providing instant information and connection.

Although we have created a huge array of life improvements with innovations in technology, science, medicine and other areas, we remain challenged in many of the basic human areas of our lives. Ironically, many of the limiting beliefs and fears of the historical Renaissance remain with us as challenges today. Our challenges motivate us to re-view and re-new our beliefs about our own human power and abilities. The time has come for us to get to know, value, and trust ourselves as creators of a new renaissance.

2
Expanding Our Vistas

We can never solve a problem from the level of thinking on which it was created.

Albert Einstein

A renaissance happens when thinking in radically different ways allows us to become aware of previously invisible options. My trip to the Grand Canyon taught me that our body/mind could re-format and even block things from view altogether, but this implied that vision could also be formatted to expand vistas. This intentional reformatting begins by adopting new expanded premises about ourselves and our world.

To begin to expand our perspective, I propose we re-view four key areas of thought and belief that shape our experience of life. These phenomena become habits of mind that can block our ability to explore. However if we open ourselves to new perspectives on these mental constructs, we expand our vistas. The first is our idea about knowledge itself.

Reframing Knowledge as Action

He who says he knows, does not know, and
He who says he does not know, does not know.

Anonymous

Expanding our awareness begins by taking a fresh look at our beliefs about knowing anything. We say that "knowledge is power." We can start to redefine that power as an active, dynamic state rather than an accumulation of facts and ideas. When viewed this way, knowledge becomes more like exploration and expansion—more about the mastery of learning itself than of knowing facts. Knowledge is more about process than product.

Of course, part of us always seeks certainty. We find safety in what we believe to be known territory: facts, data, logical proof, history, or "the ways it's always been." Our current culture keeps us from exploring unsafe new places by reinforcing our obsession with knowing things. We are trained to believe in the infallibility of what we call "facts," and we consider certain prior knowledge to be non-changing and absolute. Of course, we often find out that these beliefs are flawed, yet we return again and again to that safe harbor.

Our consensus system tells us that the more knowledge one has, the more valuable one becomes, especially if that knowledge has been certified by a university or other credible organization. Someone with advanced degrees and professional designations is trusted as an expert. Over the centuries, we have placed increasing value on expertise—on those who acquire and are certified as having more specific and specialized knowledge. And while expertise is valuable, we want to make sure it does not limit us or prevent us from seeing new possibilities.

Our cultural obsession with knowledge as a commodity defined by what we already know can trap us in situations (like our present crises) where alternatives are needed and available, but we are not open to discover them.

Throughout this book, I propose that a key skill for our renaissance is our ability to perceive the world from a variety of perspectives simultaneously, while not sacrificing our ability to focus on everyday life. What I am suggesting might be called higher-level multitasking, and I am quite sure that many people do it now. The Renaissance person is aware of and trained to use an expanded skill set. This will be a key difference from the way most people function now.

A new world is always un-known to the conscious mind, which relies on proven, safe models. Thus the unknown, and all it represents, carries a huge charge of fear. So it makes sense that the moment we begin to open ourselves to unknown thoughts, emotions, or experiences, an entire suite of fear-based reactions kicks in, geared to stop us before "we make a mistake" or "get into trouble," or worse. This very primal, deep, and largely unconscious response program is complex. It is an innate asset, designed for our protection; however, it can be erroneously triggered by many of the stressors in our modern world. Our fear of the unknown can also be used to manipulate or control us.

Because a renaissance moves us out into the unknown, understanding how we may react to exploring new ideas or behaviors can be the key to opening new worlds. Once we become more aware of our own inner processes, we have already made a shift in the direction of a renewed self and a new world. In an old cartoon strip called *Pogo*, the main character, Pogo, once declared that "we have met the Enemy, and he is us!"[4] If we can accept this truth and look ourselves in the eye with openness and love, we can re-view and re-new.

I suggest we redefine "unknown" as "new" or not yet realized, and replace our fear reaction to it with one of excitement and curiosity. Knowing takes on a new meaning when we perceive it as an act of exploration and discovery. Knowing becomes an active, fluid vehicle instead of a passive, rigid repository. In this sense, we use our suite of invisible tools to know about ourselves, or any part of the universal consciousness, as well as to grow and create continuously.

Years ago, one of my mentors in the field of organizational development shared an insight about knowledge that has helped me throughout life. We were discussing organizational communication process, and the ways in which it can become dysfunctional when people consciously or unconsciously conceal information. My mentor, Bob, looked at me seriously and said, "Clare, if you forget everything else about organizations, remember this: at any moment, on any day, in any organization, anyplace on this earth, *everybody knows everything*. If you think they don't, you are wrong. Remember this, and you will do well."[5]

Bob's Law: *Everybody knows everything.*

Time and time again, I have found that he was right. I began to call this principle Bob's Law. People are never really fooled by attempts to conceal information, because we all possess sophisticated detection equipment that works 24/7. Although people may not immediately understand what is causing their discomfort, they will guess, gossip, and try to figure it out. One common example of Bob's Law is the love affair that coworkers believe they are concealing. Of course, everyone has known about it since day one. When people are ill, everyone knows. When they are angry, sad, or dissatisfied with their job, everyone knows. Most importantly, Bob's Law can be used to create more productive human environments.

Most people spend the majority of their life in the workplace so organizations provide a crucial context for renaissance work. In years of coaching, I have had the opportunity to assist leaders in understanding how using Bob's Law and renaissance skills can help them be more effective. As Queen Elizabeth I knew, a leader is always on stage. Because of this, leaders have the opportunity to effect change by personally modeling all the values, norms, and behaviors they wish to see reflected in the organization.

Leaders can learn to use what we might call intentional *being,* to marshal all visible and invisible channels to transmit positive messages. To be most effective, a leader must not simply speak or act in certain ways, but intend and believe – really BE the substance of their messages. If the intentional/belief piece is missing, everyone will know it! You can't fake authenticity. How many times have we experienced or heard about the organizational "talking head"? People are not fooled.

To be authentic, leaders must take the time to first know and develop themselves, learning to know and use more of their own inner power. Their ability to clearly communicate expectations, goals, and direction that speaks to people relies on their willingness to do the hard work first of understanding themselves, their vision, and overcoming as many of their own blocks as possible. I find that if the hard work of understanding and articulating is done up front, there is seldom an issue with crafting effective messages. I always liken this to the work involved in painting a room. The taping of the woodwork and windows takes forever, but once done well, the paint goes on fast and perfectly. The leader's internal preparation, or taping, always pays human capital dividends. His or her hard work also prepares them to make it look easy to those around them.

Once leaders do the internal work to understand, articulate, and focus their power, they transmit vision and messages even without words—like a continuous broadcast signal. Effective, clear intention allows one to send a message by just being in a room.

An additional workplace bonus of Bob's Law is that once you know it, you also understand how to cut down on wasted employee time, energy, and goodwill: communicate as clearly as possible! It pays real dividends to create environments where clear, open communication is the norm regarding an organization's goals, expectations, feedback, and appreciation of excellence.

Also, we might try asking people what they do know. We can learn much about what messages we are actually sending to our organizations, and if there is dissonance with our stated goals and values. Think how much time and misunderstanding we might also avoid if we acknowledged people's intuitive skills and valued them as resources.

Demystifying our extra-ordinary capabilities is key to our renaissance.

The importance of Bob's Law in everyday life is that we all come with the innate ability to know anything and everything. That idea is a renaissance in itself. It's a Grand Canyon-sized concept that can create proportionately huge new outcomes. We just have to re-discover that innate knowledge process. Providing more people with clear information, language, and tools for this discovery might be all we need to facilitate dramatic changes.

Expansion: Living Larger

Because expanded awareness facilitates discovery, it makes sense to look at some of the ways expansion and its opposite, contraction, function. Certainly, both functions are normal and necessary. For example, our lungs expand when we take in air/oxygen, but they must contract for us to expel the CO_2. That is one level of what one might call functional expansion and contraction. To see new options, we can look at the way various ideas about expanding or contracting may limit our current field of possibilities.

Every time we say or hear phrases like "that's just the way it is," "it is what it is," "we have always done it this way," or my favorite "we already discussed this," we contract our field of possibility. Such contraction also keeps us stuck in the zone of the known, in our comfort zone.

Contraction becomes a habit of mind that we value in the field of knowledge. Our high value on specialization creates ever-contracting circles of focus, turning specialists into experts, a word which carries a positive connotation. Meanwhile a person who casts his net wider might be called "a jack-of-all-trades and master of none," which carries a more negative connotation.

Seen from a different angle, an expansive person may carry the more positive title of Renaissance Man, but chances are that society rewards him (or her) for a certain specialty, then admires that he demonstrates other skills and talents. Additionally, the Renaissance Man's very name implies a connection with that almost mythical by-gone era; he is someone who is rare, not a normal person.

We can see that the conflicting implications of the term Renaissance Man reveal our ongoing ambivalence about human power. Although society publicly applauds certain famous explorers, artists, or innovators, they are portrayed as unique, extra-ordinary. In addition, the gender-specific term Renaissance Man tells us even more – these special people are men! The literal and connotative meanings of the term work together to exclude most people and all women.

We may say that we aspire to expansion, to thinking outside the box, but we often dismiss, ridicule, or fire the people who actually do it. In everyday settings, people are often censured for too much exploring, questioning, or innovating. Because of this, people learn that it is safest to stay within the sanctioned limits to get along in the world. Stay safe; don't make waves. Best to leave exploration and innovation to those special people who are great. Of course, we know this is baloney.

Every person is a Renaissance Person.

Another useful perspective on the expansion/contraction phenomenon comes from quantum physics, which tells us that the field of being at any one time contains both particles and waves. The particle is like the contracted focus, not frozen, but subject to change by a dynamic but sequential process. It is the expansive wave aspect that allows for the instant "quantum shift" of substance—miracles happen in the wave. Therefore, exploring and discovering more about expansion could be very beneficial.

We can explore other aspects of these fundamental principles. One important consideration is that contraction is a natural and even physical response to fear. As we have noted many times, healthy fear is good, but our human race—especially in what we call civilized society—is based on many fear programs that manipulate and abuse our innate fear instincts. The daily stress or fear levels are so high that many people live in a continuous state of contraction. The mind contracts, the focus narrows, the whole body mechanism contracts—muscles, blood vessels, vision, breath, and on and on.

Further, as we age, we seem to contract. Isn't it common knowledge that as one ages, one gets shorter? People seem to curl up into themselves as if returning to the comforting fetal position. It may be that this process is the result of living in fear and without healthy habits for so many years that momentum just takes over. If you look at an active athlete in their seventies, eighties, or beyond (think of the famous Jack LaLanne or Paul Bragg), they remain straight, open, and expanded. Such folks look pretty good until their death. They gave themselves permission to expand—mentally and physically, based on their culturally-authorized commitment to fitness and their status as a fitness authority. The regular person is usually not so lucky.

If we accept for a moment that natural, useful expansion and contraction (such as that of muscles, the lungs, swelling and shrinking of material in response to heat and cold) is a working principle of life in our world, we can begin to discern what types of contraction we might want to manage better or even delete from our programs, and what types of expansion we might want to install as regular functions. Of course, by even thinking about this topic, you have already expanded!

As we reconsider our human capabilities throughout this book, we will continue to explore the concepts of expansion and contraction. In our journey of discovery we are re-training our perception to new levels of discernment in many areas we now take for granted.

"What You Resist, Persists": The Power of Polarity

Everyone has probably heard the phrase quoted above, and at some level we have all experienced its truth. The novelty toy called Chinese handcuffs provides a good metaphor for this—the harder you pull away, the tighter they get.

We hold our limiting beliefs or worries steadfastly in place by this simple rule. Think for just a second of all the advertising phrases based on resistance: "anti-aging," "wrinkle fighters" and "wars" on crime, drugs, or poverty. By doing this, we keep in place exactly what we claim to want to delete. Once we become aware of the polarity phenomenon, and the way it functions, we can detect where it might be limiting our power, keeping us in patterns we do not desire. We can begin to delete or better manage this feature in our own lives rather than taking unconscious ownership of the many "anti" campaigns that may lock us into undesirable states. I observe two general **polarity principles:**

1. Any concept or belief that is invoked by name has manifested through the act of naming it. The energy, frequency, and whole history of a concept, like aging, are contained within the word.

2. The effect of Rule 1 actually *gains strength* when one tries to negate it by using a negative prefix. This is because the energy of the negative creates an opposition - a polarity that holds the thing in place, like the attractive force between two opposing magnetic poles.

The popular New Age maxim, "Universe does not hear negatives," ironically demonstrates how the principle works. The popular advice has been to create and use positive affirmations to change one's perspective and aspects of life. An affirmation is stated in the positive, of course, such as "I am successful in my business," or "My business is abundant." However, even a positive statement may trigger the polarity trap if underlying negative beliefs have not been detected and released. Shouting that positive thing over and over might make things worse, if the motivation is really "I will NOT fail in my business," or "I refuse to fail."

Just as the harder we push back to an idea, concept, or person, the more we hold them in place, the more forceful we are about our positive declarations, the more resistance may be lurking under the surface. We may not realize how much internal resistance we have to something we desire. The force of our affirmation will reveal it—if we find ourselves arguing it, pushing it, almost protesting it, there is polarity there.

We probably all know someone who is constantly delivering what I call the progress report. Every time we speak to them, they launch into a forceful declaration of all that they are doing, accomplishing, and manifesting. Their report usually has an undertone of stress, a polarity of pushback. After listening to others deliver these reports for years, and also hearing myself deliver them, I believe that this type of affirmation is powered not by a positive belief, but by fear that all this might NOT be true. Without the polarity of fear, the forceful declarations would probably not be needed, and the desired state would manifest more quickly.

I recently had a very clear understanding of this phenomenon. I had become frustrated with a chronic health issue, and had slipped into a battle with it. I was vacillating between traditional allopathic doctors, alternative professionals, and my own methods, but nothing seemed to work. I began to question my belief in the whole realm of alternative health, but more importantly, I began to doubt my body's own power to be healthy. My ego was also bruised—the issue became an emblem of personal failure.

One weekend, I just got fed up. I yelled at God, myself, and my teachers and mentors and declared, "I am going to go into meditation now. And damn it! I want the answer! This is enough. I can no longer operate this way." I went into a meditation and realized that this resistance was not only holding this issue in place, it was strengthening it! I heard a voice say, *"Drop the charges! Healing takes place in a neutral space—you know that. The space of Love has no resistance. Detect your areas of resistance and let them go—you will be fine."*

I thought I was pretty advanced, of course, so it was humbling to recognize once again that detecting and engaging with areas of resistance in my body was a very sophisticated skill. To make matters worse, I realized that my own unknown thoughts and beliefs were in the way. Further, I had to let go of thinking at all, especially in the analytical, goal-oriented way we are taught.

First, I addressed the anger and judgment of myself for not handling the whole thing better. Instead, I began to just be present with my body, letting messages and feelings come up, verbally or not, and giving them space to express without labeling them as bad, wrong, or sick. As much as I could, I sent waves of unconditional love to myself and to anyone else suffering from something like this.

As I continued this work, the pain subsided. As I kept up the practice over days, the issue began to resolve. I reached out for help from professionals, but I focused my energy and theirs differently. This was an inside job, and only I could shift its terms of operation. I had to get into the driver's seat and practice that paradoxical operation of control by release. I needed to let go and stop fighting the invisible enemy that was *me* all along!

My revelation showed me that I was resisting in more ways than I thought. I was not only just pushing back to having the problem and wanting it gone, I was pitting traditional against alternative methods of dealing with it. I was also comparing myself to friends of mine with similar issues who had dealt with them in certain ways, and I was comparing the issue at this stage in my life to other stages of my life—even invoking resistance to my own beliefs about aging.

Additionally, I was angry—at all of it! Anger signals huge resistance. I was mostly angry at myself. Instead of accepting my issue and understanding it, listening to its message, I was just mad at it and thus holding it in place indefinitely. I was resisting and it was persisting.

When we remove our resistance, we neutralize the polarity that holds problems in place.

I may always have to remind myself to "drop the charges" of resistance—in all of its forms. The play on the word "charge" has also caused me to look in new ways at other possible meanings of "charging" or "filing charges." With my expanding awareness, language became an expanded resource.

Whenever polarity troubles me, I remember my favorite science fiction hero, Doctor Who.[6] Doctor Who had a "sonic screwdriver," which he used as his first tool of choice when he encountered one of his typical dramatic emergencies in unknown frontiers of space/time. He used the screwdriver to "reverse the polarity," and often that would fix the whole emergency. When we drop the charges on an issue, we are using our own sonic screwdriver, which proves to be a useful tool.

For example, I struggled with the polarity of anger and frustration with a greedy figure involved in harmful political tactics within my community. To resolve things, a friend advised me to use a sonic screwdriver tactic: to meditate every day and visualize this person having everything they desired. This was the opposite of what I had been doing, thinking up ways to thwart the person's maneuvers and desired outcomes. My friend helped me to realize that my resistance was helping to hold the unwanted energy firmly in place.

Reverse polarity tools have been used for years in professional communication to shift the terms of a difficult interpersonal engagement and "re-frame" it for a new outcome. Negotiation training provides an excellent example. In his classic work, *Getting Past No*, William Ury has a chapter entitled "To Change the Game, Change the Frame," which he opens by advising that to reframe an adversarial negotiation, we should "do the opposite of what you may feel tempted to do. Treat your opponent like a partner. Instead of rejecting what your opponent says, accept it—and reframe it as an opportunity to talk about the problem."[7] Sales training focuses on similar techniques of partnering with the potential customer, establishing common ground around benefits and reducing polarity-charged objections about cost.

The idea of polarity reversal is also fundamental to martial arts—one does not battle *against* an opponent, one steps *into* his aggressive energy and makes use of it. Techniques of sitting meditation also involve staying with thoughts or discomfort that one would normally fight or escape, just "being" with the internal "enemy" until one understands and engages with its power. The charge of any polarized issue or engagement produces tremendous power that can be harnessed best by releasing the energy spent fighting it. Once I began to investigate the many ways polarity tools were useful, I discovered a huge new resource that I could apply to almost every activity in my life.

POLARITY REVERSAL EXERCISE

To practice using your version of the sonic screwdriver, you can try the following exercise:

1. **Identify the resistance,** polarity, or charge that you have to any person or issue. For example, maybe you are angry about having to do something at work. Take a moment and allow yourself to FEEL the ways in which you are resisting this task or what it represents to you. See if you can make a quick list of all the ways you are pushing back.
2. **Consciously release as much resistance as possible**. Do this as specifically as possible, and use language to make it real. You can say, for example, "I release my anger about having to do this task. I forgive my boss for asking me to do it. I know that doing it is necessary and I will move into the activity and go with the flow. There must be a reason for this, and I accept it."
3. **Create a mental picture of yourself (and others) moving through the issue easily, without resistance.** You can see yourself doing the task easily, even having fun doing it. You can see your boss happy and getting what he wants because you did the task.
4. **Then go forward with your activity and day.** Be aware of your shift and keep your new attitude. Enjoy your new freedom to experience the activity with no resistance. See what happens.

This exercise can be challenging because it runs counter to most of what we have been taught, so when you first start to do it, it feels wrong. But it works. It frees us up to actually be present, so we also perform better and make everyone happier.

A friend who is a professional pilot recently wrote to me that he had used the technique when he was required to go through a series of required trainings and qualifying tests in an atmosphere of pressure and interpersonal dissonance. He wrote that when he just gave in and even decided to enjoy the experience, everything began to go extremely well. He had reversed the polarity. He wrote, "I tried something you taught me . . . not to resist. I simply relaxed. No expectations or stress to perform. I simply did what I do best." The result was that the whole experience was so easy that he "nearly did the project with my eyes closed."

An unexpected side benefit occurred – people were attracted to his positive attitude. Everyone around him became more relaxed and positive when he did. This included the instructor, who had been at odds with my friend previously. With the polarity dropped, the instructor became supportive and said that my friend's results were "the closest perfect he had seen." He ended his message saying, "Funny how things work. As you say, 'All the things you resist, persist.' That was my guiding light." Voila. Feel free to try the technique yourself and let me know how it works!

Seeing New is Being New

> *The mind/body is not a collection of separate parts; it is a profoundly intelligent holographic system. This intelligent wholeness is the true source of our vision, and seems to be the only aspect of the mind/body that science hasn't scrutinized.*
>
> Jacob Liberman, *Take Off Your Glasses and See*

Jacob Liberman's classic work is a must-read for anyone interested in exploring the renaissance activity of re-vision.[8] We can relearn the many ways our "intelligent wholeness" sees things that have previously been invisible. We have come to be highly visual beings, using our eyesight much more than other species, and more than our ancestors did. We need a new kind of vision to see new worlds.

We get into the habit of relying on our eyesight, which we call vision, to tell us what is real in the external world. We place a high value on correct vision, also known as 20/20 eyesight or precise acuity, which we believe gives us the best information about reality. As Liberman demonstrates, our over-reliance on two-dimensional vision—on the written word—in education, for example, contracts and limits our ability to learn with our whole body/mind and creates an entire constellation of dysfunctions. We tend to under-develop (or abuse) our other senses: hearing, smell, taste, or touch.

No formal educational system teaches us expanded use of our senses.

No wonder we have so many issues with our sensory organs as we go through the years not knowing how to use or care for them. One of my first alternative teachers, who was originally from outside the United States, observed that the average American's life goal was to "retire, get hearing aids, false teeth, bifocals, wig, fake body parts, then die." This simple observation still makes me laugh, but also conveys a sad truth. Maybe learning to use and care for all our five senses would be a start!

Of course, we also have a sense category for a type of perception we call the "sixth sense," which is usually relegated to either accidental or paranormal status. Thus our sixth sense—the ability to use our more expanded consciousness and perception package—is denied any place in education. We also devalue (or deride) its use by real people in most real-life contexts, such as business, healthcare, or other endeavors. After several decades as a consultant in the world of everyday work, I must say that most talented professionals eventually have admitted to me that they rely on some version of this expanded perception, although they may not publicly declare it.

Vision may be more about the mind than it is about the eyes.

People who are what we call "visionaries" are using an expanded capacity to see with what Shakespeare taught us to call the "mind's eye" (*Hamlet*, Act I, Scene 2, l. 186). They are tapping into imagination and the invisible realms, sort of like the shaman did to see Columbus' ships. *They are seeing something that is not yet available to everyone else.* Visionaries work in all fields of endeavor, in science, art, economics, medicine, and other areas. The visionary sees what others do not see, but may not see what the others see. In other words, this type of person has so developed their ability to expand and imagine, that the everyday world of the here-and-now may seem almost irrelevant.

To facilitate the achievement of their vision, however, they need to demonstrate and communicate the reality and relevance of their vision. They have to break through strong belief barriers that block other people's ability to share their new world view. Visionaries sometimes have to die without realizing success; then later someone else "discovers" their brilliant ideas. What if we encouraged, valued, and rewarded people, starting in early education, for learning to expand their perspective? Everyday visionaries do exist; we can acknowledge and develop them.

Great organizational leaders are often visionaries. They realize that their positional power is an opportunity to serve by leading an organization or group into a renaissance of positive change. Even though a leader may have the bully pulpit, they are not guaranteed acceptance by the rank and file, by senior people in their organization, or by their successors. Several decades of consulting with organizational leaders has taught me this firsthand.

Although specifics of my consulting work remain confidential, I can relate general facts. One impressive example of a visionary leader's dilemma took place in an ultra-conservative organization. My client, newly promoted to lead, sought to develop expanded leadership skills and vision at the management level throughout the organization. His fresh creative ideas were inspired by some of the greatest authors in leadership and organizational development, based on sound theory and successful results. The difficulty was getting traction for innovative thought and practice in an organizational culture that had so long been fixed in its own process and vision. Many could not "see" what he saw at all, much less how it applied to them or could help them do a better job. It was the Grand Canyon and Columbus' ships all over again.

Fortunately, many did benefit and value this great leader's vision and commitment to expanded human excellence. Some new methods were implemented, and many old behaviors changed; many staff members were grateful for his contribution. However, when the leader moved on, his successor brought back a more traditional approach, and some return to older ways. Change had taken place, but more time was needed to build a new consciousness and organizational norms. In time, more people could have demonstrated results that would allow senior management within the organization to support the work and the shift.

In another client organization, a leader's radically new and expanded human vision took almost a decade to succeed, but it worked! In this case, the organization was more ready for change, as it was in a chaotic period when the leader assumed her position. Because chaos causes folks to run for the safety of old habits, and fear can cause vision to block completely, the leader's path was fraught with difficulty. Her own people, the press and public pushed back, often acting as if they did not perceive at all what she was saying, writing, and doing. They had no processor for this new information.

As years went by, the leader held the positive course, and growing numbers of people "saw the ships." A solid core group within and outside the organization helped the leader to persevere and create a renaissance for her organization and a model for others. She was also able to select and develop new leadership and implement a succession plan to ensure the continuity and growth of the renaissance vision.

There is always more of the invisible, unknown world than of the one we see and know.

Luckily, people can learn to expand their vision or at least accept the existence of previously invisible phenomena. We currently accept microbes as a part of everyday reality even though we cannot see them. Folks everywhere buy hand sanitizer and use it obsessively! Not too long ago, microbes and atoms were unknown and invisible. If we can accept these phenomena and even take them for granted, what else is possible?

3
COMMANDING UNSEEN FORCES

> *We are all potential wonder workers, dormant yogis, and it is clear . . . that it would behoove us both as individuals and as a species to devote a good deal more effort into harnessing these talents.*
>
> Michael Talbot, *The Holographic Universe*

Michael Talbot first wrote the words above in 1994, just before his death. At that time, there was less valid research than we now have to support his claim. Today, however, even with all the data available, most of us still go through decades or even lifetimes as "dormant yogis." A human renaissance is about learning to awaken those dormant powers.

Just as *Star Wars* hero Luke Skywalker learned to command *the force* to succeed in his quest, we evolve on our renaissance journey through increasing awareness, exploration, and use of previously unknown power sources. Like Luke, we learn to command not only our physical body and actions, but also the powerful unseen forces within and around us. To embark on our own explorations, we need foundation principles that help us navigate.

We have already re-viewed some of these foundation principles, including Bob's Law and new ways of thinking about knowledge, expansion, polarity, and vision itself. Having opened ourselves to these ideas, we arrive at what I see as the two core premises of our human renaissance: the knowledge that we are powerful beings, and the understanding that most of our crucial resources are invisible. Let's take a look at these premises.

Human Power Premise & The 99% Invisible Rule

Two main premises form the foundation for our renaissance. I call the first premise the **Human Power Premise**.

We are powerful beings with extensive abilities that we are not trained to access or use.

This premise includes the following additional elements:

- We are like human supercomputers, possessing both physical and invisible components, programs, and tools.
- We have various interfaces or portals through which we can access, explore, use and manage the many resources of our power.
- As we recognize and use more of our powerful resources, we exponentially expand our ability to discover and create new worlds.

The second key premise is what I call the **99% Invisible Rule**.

99% of our life is supported, driven, and manipulated by invisible phenomena.

This crucial rule covers all aspects of ourselves and the vast world that we cannot perceive with untrained senses. Invisible phenomena include the inner workings of our own bodies, as well as our emotions, thoughts and memories, and energies. Also included are all the invisible phenomena of the world and universe that we perceive as outside of us: all energy, light, sound, and the vast sea of what we call consciousness.

Although these invisible phenomena comprise 99% of our active resources, our daily awareness remains fixed on the 1% of the "reality" most readily available to our senses.

We pay most attention in our daily life to the proverbial tip of the iceberg. Meanwhile, the rest of the enormous iceberg is running the show. It's time to reclaim more of our immense power. The Power Premise and the 99% Invisible Rule help us to be aware of our power resources so we can begin using them. These power resources are our birthright.

Einstein insisted throughout his life on the importance of developing our ability to see the world and its challenges from new perspectives. He knew that the solutions to our problems truly do come from within us, as we learn to access our invisible resources.

OUR INVISIBLE UNIVERSE OF POWER

> *The break with the past will come, in part, by accepting that, like light or sound, our present band of cognition gives us a window on only a very small portion of Nature's total modes of expression.*
>
> William Tiller, *Science and Human Transformation*

William Tiller's work cited above was one of my first guidebooks to the scientific study of energy, consciousness, and the way human beliefs and intentions create reality.[9] Tiller and others helped me to understand the complex realms of the invisible, and how I could actually begin to perceive more of the world. In the following sections, I present an overview of the exciting invisible resources integral to our lives.

We have all probably heard the phrase, "everything is energy." We seem to take it for granted without really thinking about details. However, the word "energy" includes a lot of possible phenomena. When people speak about energy, they can mean just a feeling they have, or measurable energetic data, like electromagnetic frequencies or radiation, or the less measurable attributes of the quantum world, or of spirituality and consciousness.

Think of all the features of our world that we cannot see but now accept as being there: energy fields, our body's electromagnetic energy, our energy flows and meridians, earth energy vortexes and lines, all types of frequency, and the entire spectrum of sound and light. Today, we have the technology to detect and measure many of these phenomena, but even before we could see them, they were there. Whenever someone tells me they "don't believe in all this energy stuff," I ask them if they can explain how their cell phone works, or how all those programs get into their TV. How about those distant servers in the "cloud"? We have no problem trusting these mysterious invisible phenomena when it comes to transmitting, receiving, and storing the most crucial information in our lives.

Perhaps the most important component of our invisible world is the energy we call consciousness. Consciousness can be defined as the creative force of sentience in our universe. We live and participate in a mostly invisible web or matrix of consciousness. This vast invisible terrain includes the ideas, thoughts, emotions, events, and all components for everything that ever was, is, or will be. Consciousness is truly limit-less. Fortunately, to engage in our renaissance, we need not comprehend the enormity of consciousness, but we do need to understand some of the working principles and techniques that can help us to access and use this vast resource.

We live and participate in a limitless invisible field of active sentience.

Many scientists—biologists, physicists, and others—have taken their turn at explaining the operational principles that underlie the invisible matrix in which we live. Scholars and researchers have produced reams of literature, and conducted uncountable experiments, in diverse professional fields: medicine, biology, physics, philosophy, and others. I'd like to briefly re-view how we have developed on our way to understanding some of these core principles of an expanded life.

NEW AGE MAPS TO THE NEW WORLD

In the last twenty or thirty years, popular literature and other media have introduced the public to aspects of our powerful consciousness matrix and to our power as human beings. They quite literally gave us the manuals and maps we were missing to rediscover ourselves and our world. Science fiction films and books, TV series, and even cartoons have long relied on principles of quantum physics and advanced consciousness techniques in their stories. *Doctor Who, The Jetsons, ET, Star Trek, Star Wars*, and many other creations brought these ideas and images into our collective mind. In the late 1980s and into the 1990s, many authors began to apply these phenomena to our real lives. Michael Talbot, Amit Goswami, Wayne Dyer, Deepak Chopra, Louise Hay, Shakti Gawain, Barbara Brennan, Fred

Alan Wolf, William Tiller, and Carolyn Myss were just some of the trailblazers of what we came to call the New Age.[10]

The New Age self-help movement gained popular momentum in the 2000s when the movies like *What the Bleep Do We Know!?* (2004) and *The Secret* (2006) described how real people can and do interact with the invisible realms of creative consciousness.[11] Today, these foundational works combine with an ever-growing number of workshops, lectures, and YouTube videos to provide information to anyone who can access the Internet.

The result is that we now have a huge body of work regarding consciousness and human power that has prepared our way and brought us to a new place. Regrettably, *the average person is still not taught about any of this.* Further, as we will see throughout the book, the majority of what we call New Age wisdom is still considered non-mainstream and even rejected by people in traditional business, healthcare, and other real-life contexts. The obvious question is: why has all of this core information remained separate from the lives of so many people?

The answer may be that although decades of now not-so-New Age literature, movies, workshops, and lectures provided maps to get us to our New World, *we were not all fully ready to believe or see it.* The dense, sturdy old beliefs and ways of the twentieth century could not be dismantled in a decade, or even two or three. A much greater mass of people had to create and join a new matrix of belief, thought, and action. This matrix can now become large enough to drive real change.

The focus of much of the New Age's ground-breaking work was how to intentionally make use of the energy of consciousness by developing our own invisible powers of thought, emotion, and belief. The result is best known as the Law of Attraction or the theory of manifestation. Manifestation is just one of the ancient techniques revived in the New Age, but its importance is crucial because it is based upon the use of our invisible tools — our thoughts, intentions, emotions, and senses — to manifest tangible results.

As most New Age authors acknowledge, manuals describing manifestation techniques are far from new. This ancient wisdom was hidden or remained undisclosed, as *The Secret* famously pointed out. Understanding and using the creative forces of consciousness has been taught by esoteric and religious mystery schools for centuries, under many names. Witchcraft has long accessed ancient manifestation recipes, as does the sacred Kabala. Look at the modern upsurge of Kabalistic study, geared toward not only spiritual goals, but the more worldly goals of financial abundance, physical health, beauty, and love. Many meditation techniques that have been modified and taught to the public often have similar goals—the use of our inner power to influence our outer world to create abundance, health, and love.

Many New Age self-help works provide techniques for manifestation. The process typically involves crafting statements called affirmations, which are intentions charged with the creative power of emotion. We might say that the recipe or formula for manifesting optimal outcomes goes something like this:

Intention + visualization + emotional charge = manifestation

Although as we will discuss later, techniques of manifestation can present complications, the basic recipe seems pretty simple. First you must state an *intention*, which is best stated positively in the present tense, as specifically as possible, as if it is already in effect. For example, say you want to manifest a new car. You state specifically what you are manifesting: "I now own a new, 2014, red Nissan Juke, fully loaded (with sunroof, all options, chrome trim, and all-wheel-drive)." Next you add the *visualization:* you visualize yourself in this car in as much detail as possible, driving it happily down the road. You see the sights from the driver's seat, you see people looking at your sporty car. You see the entire vehicle in exact detail.

Finally, you charge the visualization with *emotion*: as much as possible, you feel the happiness, the car underneath and around you, all the sensations you would enjoy about having this cute little car. Use all your senses: smell the new car scent, hear the engine, see the colors and equipment, feel the seats and steering wheel. Each component of a manifestation recipe builds on the previous one to make the intention more real. Once you have the basic recipe, you simply repeat it daily, visualizing and feeling it as if it already exists, until it shows up in 3D. Based on the now-famous Law of Attraction, you attract what you think, feel, and believe consistently.

Perhaps our most significant challenge in presenting or summarizing what we know about our invisible resources is the lack of general knowledge and consistent language to define these phenomena. For this reason, I want to share my perspective on some of the key working principles of consciousness.

We can think of the invisible field we call consciousness as data that is continuously being processed into and out of form, literally in-forming, and shifting form. In his book *Mind Into Matter,* Fred Alan Wolf includes a drawing by artist Maurits Escher, which shows two hands drawing each other into being, entitled "Information Shaping reality Shaping In-formation." Wolf comments, "As illustrated in this drawing by Escher, information and matter move continually in self-referencing interaction that forms instruction to continually transform matter, which in turn feed back information, recreating matter all over again."[12]

In his foreword to Tiller's *Science and Human Transformation,* Dr. Ernest Pecci seems to describe the same idea when he states, "There is an unseen matrix that gives form to the seen. It is in constant flow and harmony through an instantaneous exchange of information in every direction."[13] The "unseen matrix" to which Pecci refers is often called energy or the field of consciousness.

Masaru Emoto's important research on water crystals demonstrated clearly that intention, carried through any medium—sound, language or simply intention—has the power to alter what we think of as physical reality. In fact, as Emoto points out, physical and non-physical are simply aspects of energy—of vibration and frequency—that exist in a fluid, dynamic interplay in our universe. Emoto concludes, "The entire universe is in a state of vibration, and everything generates its own frequency, which is unique," thus "everything is vibration."[14] The nature and strength of any type of vibration can cause healthy or unhealthy effects in the structures of the receivers. Emoto's amazing photos of changes to water crystals when exposed to various types of vibration from sound, language, and thought demonstrate the power of this principle.

Further, as many scientists and authors have shown, similar or like frequencies attract each other based on the principle of resonance. They literally vibrate to the same rhythm. This principle of resonance is crucial to the Law of Attraction. When we employ the manifestation formula, we create an intentional frequency field that attracts whatever resonates with it or shares its nature. Further, as Emoto and others have shown, transmitting intentional vibration or frequency causes change in everything in our field. Almost everyone has probably heard stories of the peace, joy, or bliss that people experience in the presence of great spiritual masters. This is frequency transmission at work.

New Age authors and researchers help us to view ourselves as living in a limitless invisible field of creative energy that is always moving in and out of form and affecting us at many levels of being—physical and non-physical. To use this resource, we first need to know how the field works and how it impacts us. A major operational premise of consciousness fields is the way that physical or non-physical features are in-formed. When I first began my research into this immense topic, I began with quantum physics. Except for the work of Tiller, Wolf, and a few others, I was overwhelmed. I realized that I had no consistent vocabulary to describe what I somehow "knew" about all of this. I needed a translation device.

Then I found the work of biologist and prolific author Rupert Sheldrake. Sheldrake's hypotheses made sense to me because I could understand and see how they functioned in real life. Sheldrake conducted extensive research on how, beyond physical explanations like DNA or training, invisible, non-local and invisible energetic fields cause generations of beings—plants, animals, or humans—to follow the same trails at the same time each year, to know how to form identical physical features, and to behave in unchanging ways. These are well-worn, well-supported, and, most importantly, invisible habit fields. The data can literally in-form beings, either physically or behaviorally. Importantly, Sheldrake also provided a language I could use to understand and safely explore this scary, expansive realm.

Sheldrake calls the consciousness phenomenon I have termed in-formation, "causative formation." Causative formation works through a principle he calls "morphic resonance," in which any type of structures or "morphic units" are attracted to and resonate with each other, forming into "morphic fields," which in turn cause physical or non-physical features and behaviors to manifest repeatedly. Morphic fields thus result in "morphogenesis," or "the coming of being into form."[15]

Simply put, the term "morphic field" denotes an invisible consciousness field phenomenon, like a habit field, which directs behaviors, thoughts, emotions, or even physiological features of the beings (morphic units) through morphic resonance, over time in the relevant field (morphogenetic field) or matrix. Importantly, the animals, plants, or humans receiving and acting upon the information in the morphic field do so without conscious thought, and without education or training.

Although Sheldrake supplied new terminology, there was existing knowledge and research about this type of field phenomenon. The theory that behaviors could be transmitted invisibly without observable training and learning was first made popular in the "hundredth monkey" research of Watson and Blair in the 1970s.[16] These researchers described studies of macaque monkeys, which showed that a very specific washing behavior that was learned by young monkeys who watched and copied adults was suddenly observed in monkeys on a neighboring island who had no such training. According to the theory, once a certain threshold number of monkeys had learned the skill, the behavior was transmitted in the consciousness field. The entire skill set instantly downloaded to all other monkeys. Sheldrake also recounts many studies done using plants, animals, and humans that prove the efficacy of field phenomena.[17]

In-formation downloads from well-worn programs are invisibly and automatically installed in all people or beings who are members of the morphic field. For example, all ducks of a certain kind simply know the paths to fly during seasonal migrations. Humans have such behavioral programming, too. After reading Sheldrake's work, I began to pay more attention to patterns of human behavior that provided everyday demonstrations of morphic fields.

I noticed that every spring break season on the beach where I live, a particular location seemed to get disproportionately huge numbers of young beachgoers. One evening, as I went for my run on the beach, I stopped two policemen and asked them if they knew why so many kids were at that one specific place. Was something special going on there? They said there was no special event; the kids always went to that spot. One of the officers told me that when he was a teen, and even in the generation before, that was just "where we went." He added, "We just knew to go there; I don't know why." I chuckled all the way down the beach—morphic fields were even governing spring break behavior!

The strength and function of these programs seems linked to two variables: the number of beings in the field-specific matrix (like the ducks or the spring breakers), and the length of time the phenomenon has been functioning. Increasing the number of participants and the length of time the phenomena exists increases the strength of the field or matrix, which seems to make it easier for the behavior to occur and for more beings to participate automatically.

We experience examples of morphic resonance in human learning contexts as well. Teachers know that in any classroom, the learning levels of students begin to shift over time based on the interaction of the learners' (and the teacher's) minds. The more advanced students bring the lower end up—"rising tide lifts all ships," as we say. At some point, the inverse can also happen as the group matrix sort of wobbles toward an advanced understanding, often causing a well-known phenomenon called "midterm slump," which I observed during decades of teaching undergraduate and graduate students.

The midterm slump happens at about the halfway point of a semester, or maybe a bit after that, when a fair amount of new content has been assimilated. For some reason, the majority of the class, which is learning well and moving forward, seems to take a nosedive. They become less knowledgeable or less able to express what they know than they were in the first weeks. How could this be?

In my experience, it surely seems that the knowledge field reaches a saturation point, where the students who are struggling impose an invisible layer of tiredness on the ones who are more easily progressing. Additionally, the ones at the head of the class are at their own critical point, where they know just enough to get themselves confused. Instead of deepening or expanding their exploration of a subject to demonstrate mastery, they often go to new and off-base places, expanding their thought, but out of the zone of relevance to the course. It is as if they are tired, too, so they want to go somewhere new. Surely, some strong and recurrent invisible phenomenon, a type of mid-term morphic field, seems to drive this cyclical behavior.

Understanding the power of invisible consciousness fields explained many other things that bothered me. For example, I always wondered how people who never knew or saw each other seemed to come up with the same ideas. Decades of studying and conducting research in several disciplines showed me that there seemed to be no such thing as original thought.

Sure, someone might hop on an idea first and get it out there in print, but tons of folks thought about it or used it before that. Many ideas that are regarded as new represent, in the words of eighteenth century English poet Alexander Pope, "what oft was thought but ne'er so well expressed."[18] In fact, it seemed to me that the more people who had previously thought and spoken about an idea or theory, the better it held up once it was officially declared and claimed as (one of my favorite ironic terms) intellectual property by someone. The idea built strength over time, forming a foundation for itself through the various people who believed and espoused it, even if those people never met or read each other's work.

Once we understand the existence and working principles of morphic fields, we can more clearly understand the power of the invisible consciousness fields in which we live. Such fields not only govern many of our habitual actions, they may also dictate many of our beliefs and the way we see (or don't see) the world. What we call consensus reality, or consensus belief, is such a field. In order to shift this, we have to know it exists. The next step is to explore the key invisible engines that influence the field of consciousness, causing various types of manifestation in our lives.

BELIEFS AND OTHER INVISIBLE MASTERS

You'll see it when you believe it.

Wayne Dyer

Wayne Dyer's brilliant turn of the common phrase, "I'll believe it when I see it," became an iconic New Age aphorism.[19] Dyer's inversion of the terms of the well-known phrase highlights the irony of our belief about the nature of belief itself. As we have already discussed, we like to think that our senses provide dependable proof of reality. So we think "seeing is believing," even if our vision might be limited or flawed. We now know that our beliefs create invisible filters, firewalls, and directors that manipulate our vision and our experience of reality.

Most importantly, Dyer's phrase asks us to consider not only how our beliefs affect or filter our ability to see the world, but how beliefs actually *create* our world. Beliefs are one of the invisible master forces that create our experience of life, and work within the field of consciousness to create our reality. *The life-changing shift of perspective is this: what if there is NO objective, external reality?* Even if you don't believe it, imagine for a moment that all of our individual and collective (invisible) thoughts, intentions, desires and beliefs, and even the act of our observation—all these unseen forces—create our lives.

This immense and shocking idea is of course the subject of much study, scholarship and controversy.[20] However, it also forms the foundation for the New Age reprisal of ancient wisdom, and a flotilla of popular self-help works in all media. If we accept the idea of a field of invisible sentience, no matter what we call it, and if we are inclined to believe in concepts like manifestation and the workings of morphic resonance and fields, then it makes sense to explore the role of belief, thought and intention.

Because beliefs are so important, I want to address them specifically. Actually knowing the breadth and depth of our beliefs is challenging, because most lie deep under the level of our awareness. Given this challenge, developing the ability to identify and modify any of our beliefs puts us ahead of the game, providing new opportunities to change our lives.

Beliefs are creative forces that invisibly drive our thoughts, behaviors, and health.

Each of us carries beliefs from our collective human experience and those that are unique to our cultures, families, and individual experiences. All the beliefs interplay and collaborate or conflict, so they take on their own dynamics that affect our being and all that we create throughout life. We may never dig deep enough to reveal all our beliefs, and knowing them might not even be desirable.

However, as we learn more about ourselves, the more we can discover about our beliefs.

Knowing that beliefs can create reality is crucial to a renaissance. But what is a belief and why does it have such power? We can define a belief as an idea or thought about the self, others and/or the world that derives power from emotions and emotional associations held over time, often by many generations of people. Beliefs operate as morphic thought fields, gaining strength over the years through shared resonance. The key is that the beliefs are usually not officially stated or learned, but are operational as governing factors in people's thoughts, behaviors, and life experience.

New Age literature helped us to understand the power of all thoughts to create reality. As Lynn McTaggart states in the introduction to her book *The Intention Experiment* (2007), "Evidence suggests that human thoughts and intentions are an actual physical "something" with the astonishing power to change our world. Every thought we have is tangible energy with the power to transform."[21] A belief is a thought on steroids, as they say. Beliefs are like turbo-charged thoughts.

Beliefs become more powerful the more people share them, the more emotional power they hold, and the longer they have been in place.

Gregg Braden explores the topic in his book *The Spontaneous Healing of Belief* (2008), where he asserts that "belief codes" underlie the workings of "the Universe as Consciousness Computer." Braden states, "Beliefs, and the feelings that we have about them, are the language that "speaks" to the quantum stuff that makes our reality."[22] Braden, Tiller, Sheldrake, Dyer, Wolf, and others all demonstrate the power of our deeply held ideas—intentions and beliefs—to create health or disease, a happy or a challenging life.

As with any morphic field, the more beings involved in a belief or belief system and the longer they hold the beliefs, the stronger the associated habitual patterning becomes. As we have seen, such patterns influence all beings whether or not they are aware of the field, or whether or not they consciously share the beliefs. In fact, the strongest programs are those that run at the deepest and least readily accessible levels of consciousness, the sub- or un-conscious levels.

Beliefs and belief systems form matrixes that we can also use intentionally to enhance our lives and health. This principle of an intentional group matrix has been taught since ancient times and is used in most courses focused on helping people achieve health and wealth. In the early twentieth century, Napoleon Hill taught the formation and use of a Master Mind group to support one's goals using the power of the like-minded, intentionally-created matrix.[23] Hill was one of the best-known early twentieth century authorities on manifestation of abundance through intentional modification of beliefs.

In his seminars, John Veltheim, founder of BodyTalk, calls an intentionally created belief matrix a "consciousness overlay."[24] BodyTalk and other well-established alternative healthcare organizations have created their own matrixes or consciousness overlay groups. Taken as a collective, all of these alternative matrixes act to soften the consensus reality firewall. The positive result is that access to new frontiers becomes easier for anyone who explores alternative health or expanded human abilities.

For most of us, the many consensus beliefs already in place dictate the ways we conduct our lives and how we experience reality. Once we become aware of their force in our lives, we can appreciate the enormity of this consensus reality iceberg. There are perhaps hundreds of belief programs invisibly operating, until they surface or appear through interfaces, such as our body or our external world. Even when they do appear, we often cannot see or translate them. This becomes especially important when we realize how much this invisible agent affects our health.

Our beliefs send continuous commands to our body that determine the state of our health.

Many researchers and authors have shown the important role that beliefs play in creating positive or negative health changes. As religious faith healers and others have known for centuries, belief heals. Belief can also harm, which is where curses get their power. If an individual believes that another's words can cause a negative or positive physical result – it will be so! In fact, many people staunchly avoid medical diagnoses, seeing them as a type of "medical cursing." With no disrespect, it is an idea worth pondering. As I write this, I do not know of any studies on the effects of diagnoses on health outcomes, but I am sure some research likely exists.

Beliefs also alter the very structure of our DNA. This effect of beliefs is being explored in the growing field of genetics called epigenetics. Books such as Bruce Lipton's *The Biology of Belief* or Dawson Church's *Genie in Your Genes* can provide good starting places for exploration of this exciting area.[25] The field of energy psychology provides crucial information and techniques for accessing and shifting stubborn beliefs that reside well below our normal awareness, but can cause life-threatening dis-ease.[26] Results of years of research in these areas demonstrate the impressive power of belief as a driver of our health at all levels.

Excavating our existing beliefs – healthy or unhealthy - is an ongoing exercise. I have found that a number of alternative modalities can help to uncover unconscious beliefs. Emotional Freedom Technique (EFT) is one I like to use.[27] Often, as I am doing an EFT tapping session, I will just talk continuously to myself, allowing myself to say anything and everything that comes to mind, and I am astonished at what can bubble up. For example, I had deep unconscious anger after the deaths of my parents. When tapping out some physical pain I was experiencing, I found myself saying things like, "They had no right to leave me," and "How could they do this after all I did for them?" I even found myself almost growling! This was a huge wake-up call. I was then able to sit down and write out a list of possible beliefs that might underlie this powerful anger. Then I tapped those out to shift them, and replaced them with more positive affirmative thoughts.

Other modalities have excellent techniques for discovering and shifting beliefs as well. The energy psychology modality called PSYCH-K has become popular with many alternative therapists. This modality uses muscle testing to locate problematic beliefs at the subconscious levels, then shifts the beliefs using affirmations combined with specific body points. Theta Healing is another resource. A Theta session typically involves quite a good deal of this digging work to discover core beliefs. The Theta facilitator works with the client to craft the appropriate replacement statements to shift problematic beliefs. BodyTalk uses a variety of process tools to work with a client's innate wisdom to locate troublesome beliefs and rebalance the body/mind. Other modalities, such as Resonance Repatterning, also have excellent techniques to assist with belief reprogramming.[28] You can explore any of these resources to see what works for you. Doing this work is truly life-changing.

Part Two

Portals to Power

Introduction

The more I studied the huge world of invisible resources, the more I realized how much in-formation and power were part of me and available to me. My body/mind and the whole world around me functioned as portals for discovery and creation. If I could expand my awareness and abilities, I could discover unlimited new things. I could also learn to better control incoming and outgoing data for optimal health and effectiveness.

The concept of an interface made sense to me, because I could easily see how it worked with my computer. I have very little idea what is in the mysterious box called my computer. I access all the goodies by switching on my monitor and interacting with icons and tools to access the programs and capabilities of the machine. Without an interface device, the box is useless to me. My PC screen interface acts as a portal that allows me to access and manipulate data that would otherwise remain invisible and unavailable.

If, like our computers, we each came with a manual at birth, it would describe our mostly invisible operating system, how our hard drive and processor worked, what programs came preinstalled, how to install or uninstall programs, and how to use our monitor interface—screen, toolbars, menus, and so on. Unfortunately, no comprehensive manual exists, so we have spent many centuries discovering or re-membering the details of our best-kept power secret: ourselves.

We lack a user manual for our complex human equipment package.

We possess a dazzling array of original or innate components, which comprise our physical and non-physical being and all our capabilities. This elegant system comes installed at birth and includes our physical body's working parts and systems, as well as invisible components such as our senses, emotions, thoughts, mind, and awareness itself. Also included here would be the components of our invisible energetic being: meridians, chakras, our energetic field, and all our frequencies.

Like our PCs, we also have what I often call programs, both innate and installed. Programs drive us to stay alive, think, feel, and act in certain ways. Innate programs include our survival mechanisms, autonomic system drivers, and innate emotional responses. Installed programs such as beliefs or belief systems can override our innate programs. As we saw in our review of consciousness fields and beliefs, these programs can be installed below the level of awareness by culture, family, religion, education, or media.

Finally, just like our computer monitors, we use various interfaces—ourselves and the entire world around us—to access our data, programs, and messages. Our primary internal interface is our entire body/mind: our physical body and all the invisible components—emotional, mental (consciousness), and spiritual (higher consciousness), which facilitate our experience of ourselves and the world.

Humans and all life-forms operate continuously as interface systems that receive, transmit, display, and manipulate data. The data comes from many places: from within our bodies, from other beings, from the environment, and from the boundless sea of consciousness. In addition to receiving and transmitting, our body/mind acts as a translator of the billions of bits of data that flow through and within us all the time. We are transformers and translators that operate with almost unimaginable complexity and elegance.

Our biological computer still rivals any machine we can create.

Discovering our body/mind information system is analogous to accessing e-mail after an extended vacation. I remember my old PC used to tell me, "You've got mail!" When I first discovered and began to access more of my innate systems, I had about forty years of mail.

Three main interface systems function as key portals to discovering many aspects of human power. The body/mind facilitates our daily life experience and acts as our primary power system. The second interface is the external world—all the things that happen around us in our lives. Last, but hardly least, is our earth itself, with all her many powerful portals. In the following chapters, we will explore each of these rich resources.

4

The Body: Our Primary Power Portal

The human body is an incredible wisdom-filled vehicle for the unfolding of the human spirit.

Thomas Cowan, *The Fourfold Path to Healing*

Our physical body represents perhaps our most familiar and readily accessible portal to power. However, as I have surely learned, our bodies comprise and access vaster frontiers than we may currently know. The physical body acts as interface not only for our physical features—organs, systems, body parts, chemistry, and the like—but also for a complex invisible system, which includes emotional, mental, and supramental or consciousness features, our huge, 99%-invisible database. Thus, the body has come to be called the "body/mind," or the physical body plus all of our invisible attributes.

Our bodies are so much more complex and expansive than our physical or chemical components, and our physical body is the access and messaging device for all our invisible components. Even with more information available now about our body/mind, most of us tend to take our marvelous machine for granted. We use our complex, elegant equipment daily with very little training. We have been taught to treat our bodies the same way we treat a machine—like a car that one takes to the shop because one cannot know the mystery within. In contrast, holistic and alternative healthcare have long proposed many valid ways to understand the language of the body.

Current self-help literature and courses in alternative modalities provide many methods and techniques to get in touch with our bodies' capabilities. Our challenge is to "connect the dots" of all of these seemingly disparate modalities to see the whole world of ourselves. We need ways to be able to use this information without becoming overwhelmed and just giving up—the way I felt about ancient Greek. We can learn the language of our bodies.

Our bodies provide an amazing array of resources and tools to maintain health. Many of these resources are invisible.

Almost forty years ago, Dr. John Diamond, a pioneer author in holistic or alternative health, wrote a brief influential book entitled *Your Body Doesn't Lie*, inspired by the work of his mentor, Dr. George Goodheart, who introduced applied kinesiology (AK) to the medical community.[1] Applied kinesiology tests specific muscles of the body to determine strength or weakness in the related organs and energetic meridians. Diamond's book uses the foundation principles of AK to demonstrate how our bodies constantly tell us about the nature and quality of our health. Since then, many health books and courses have relied on this foundation work, but the basic concepts remain constant.

Our body speaks to us continuously throughout life, and we can develop more awareness to access the information. The messages from the body regarding health or dis-ease are not recognized by most of us. If messages from the body are unheard or incompletely understood, the body may escalate the volume of symptoms to drastic, painful, or life-threatening levels to get our attention. Many of us have come to call our body messages "issues in the tissues."

It is also important to remember that our bodies are at least seventy percent water. Masaro Emoto's brilliant research demonstrating the consciousness of water underscores the crucial significance of this striking discovery for our health. His work clearly demonstrates the dramatic physical changes to water molecules caused by non-physical frequencies of music, language, or even silent intention. We know that we receive messages from ourselves and others all day long that affect our bodies at many levels we may not perceive until physical symptoms occur. Emoto also shows that in any body of water (no pun) messages are delivered to all molecules rapidly, making water an amazing medium for transmission, a tool for sending, receiving, and detecting messages.[2] Our bodies' own oceans of water provide a complete and complex information system.

We face the invisible frontier of ourselves with understandable trepidation. We are untrained in the nature and use of our own capabilities; instead, we are taught to rely on experts to understand ourselves. Actually, though, each person's own body/mind tells the truth about all levels of health. The tricky bit is learning a sound access technique to make use of our body/mind wisdom.

When we learn techniques to access our own body/mind systems, we optimize our power.

Body/Mind Components

Because the body/mind system is so complex, it makes sense to define our suite of body/mind components before we explore some key features of this primary interface. Explanations and descriptions of many of our human components are available now in any number of books, websites, and in seminars and workshops. When I began my journey thirty years ago, this was not the case.

The huge amount and scope of current information about our invisible components and abilities presents a daunting frontier for most people. Further, full disclosure and comprehensive information about our human components is not included as part of any standard educational process. For these and other reasons, most people do not incorporate this expanded view of themselves as part of their self-care, nor do they make use of the features in their own life.

I divide our fundamental physical and non-physical (or invisible) components into three categories, all of which are included under the umbrella of what we call energy.

The first category represents what most of us probably think of when we think of our body. These are physical components that we can touch and see in 3D, or if invisible to us under normal circumstances, can be seen and measured using existing technology. These components include:

- All parts of our body, including
    - Organs and endocrine glands
    - Skin, tissues, fascia
    - Body systems: blood, lymph, nerves, bones, muscles
- All body chemistry features including microbes, toxins, PH levels, hormones, minerals, and all substances that can be detected or measured in the body
- Measurable electromagnetic energy from the body, such as that emitted by the heart or brain

The second category includes energetic components, which are invisible to most of us but are accepted and used in health systems such as traditional Chinese medicine and Ayurveda. Diagrams of these body systems are readily available on the Internet. Many of these components can be viewed either with special equipment or by special individuals. This group includes:

- Chakras (energy intake, transformation, and coordination points)
- Meridians (energy lines associated with organs and functions)
- All electromagnetic, frequency, or energy fields, flows, or lines

The third category of body/mind components includes those that are the most difficult or impossible to see but are crucial to our life experience. They include:

- Consciousness (we can think of this as an expanded level of mind)
- Thoughts, ideas (we think of this as our everyday working mind)
- Emotions
- More subtle energetic fields and invisible components we currently know only as conceptual. This would include morphic fields and all quantum phenomena like quarks or soliton waves, and geometric or mathematic phenomena (like the golden mean ratio) that operate invisibly as governing phenomena.

When we expand our view of ourselves to include the invisible realms of our mind, thoughts, emotions, and energies—then go even further to include all of consciousness—we get a very different picture. The enormity of this new perspective can make it difficult to reformat our view of ourselves. Yet we do have data to help our logical mind build structures for understanding a new, expanded self. We can learn from studies like Emoto's, Lipton's, Sheldrake's, and others that all living beings communicate at cellular levels through the invisible fields of consciousness. We can also begin to explore the invisible features of our world and ourselves and discover them anew. These discoveries are the keys to our renaissance.

The more we access our invisible features, the more we realize that they are trying to access *us!*

Because we are not taught in any formal education about the less visible aspects of our bodies, we have to seek elsewhere for basic knowledge of our own equipment. This puts us in a position of vulnerability and stress, as we must always locate (and pay for) an expert to translate a language that is natural to our bodies.

An early experience taught me about the dilemma of reliance on experts, and depressed me for months. I had written a short article on part of John Milton's poem "Lycidas" for a literary journal, which I was about ready to submit.[3] In the essay, I cited a poetic fragment by the ancient Greek poet Pindar. Only a few examples of ancient Greek poetry exist, and translations of this fragment varied. Because I did not know ancient Greek, I went to an older professor who was an expert in the field and asked him for an opinion of which translation was closest to Pindar's meaning.

The professor looked at the words and sighed. Then, peering over his glasses and the piles of papers and open books on his desk, he said, "You know, Clare, you really need to learn ancient Greek to do work like this." This really frustrated me. I told him I didn't have the time to do that in the next few days just to get this thing out, so that's why I had come to him. He then kindly gave me his translation, which was luckily close to the one I favored to support my thesis. As I left, he advised, "Just remember that if you don't learn this language yourself, you will always have to rely on old fellows like me, and trust that we are right." Although learning ancient Greek never made my priority list, the experience was useful. I realized that we rely on a daunting array of experts to translate meaning from all aspects of ourselves because we are not trained to do so.

We can learn the language of ourselves.

As I studied more about invisible phenomena and about my own body, mind, and emotions, I became aware that my body/mind presented a challenging language frontier. I had so many messages from so many sources, in so many formats. I certainly had not been trained to understand my body/mind's language, how to use my own resources to translate, or when to reach out appropriately for help from an expert. Given these challenges, I began to understand better why we often feel a lack of power.

LEARNING THE BODY'S MESSAGE SYSTEM

The body often provides dramatic demonstrations of its many invisible components. Our renaissance training will help us to become more aware of this, and educate our children to better understand and use the immense resource of the body's messaging system.

When I was growing up, the prevailing consensus reality viewed the body as a sort of mechanical piece of equipment, which one took to experts for repairs. For many, that reality has not changed. Certain signals from the body—a fever, emotional distress, pains, and so on—were correctly interpreted as signs of dis-ease, but the messages could only be interpreted by an expert: the doctor. The doctor's translation toolkit was biased toward a differential diagnosis—focused on a premise that some disease was present and "ruling out" symptoms of various known maladies. We had no model that included the existence of healthy or normal dis-ease signals. We really had no model for health!

Whenever I became ill during childhood, my body's dis-ease signals were interpreted as malfunctions that needed correction, instead of as processes needing to be understood or guided through a course. Whereas before the 1950s there were not many remedies that could create almost instant health, a host of new instant-acting drugs had become available. New antibiotics—my mother called them "wonder drugs"—could create almost instant wellness, shortening illness and preventing deaths that used to be common. Unfortunately, many of my generation suffered from the administration of these wonder drugs, as our own immune systems were compromised, and many of us suffered later in life from too much of that good thing.

When a body malfunction had no clear medical diagnosis, there was (and still is to some extent) no accepted practice for asking the body what might be happening. For example, at about six, I fell down one day at camp and passed out. When I awoke, I was back in my own bed, unable to stand or walk. This disability lasted about two months, until one day I was able, with help, to walk and began rehabilitating. Although my doctor determined it was not polio (I previously had the vaccine—could that have been it?), no diagnosis was ever rendered. After studying alternative healthcare for thirty years, I now know there are many sound methods for asking the body/mind questions and determining priorities. I wonder what would have happened if someone had known how to ask my body for her messages at the time of the event.

As I went on through my teens and twenties, I developed various dis-ease triggers as a response to stress or mental or emotional imbalances. But because I was not taught to perceive my body's messaging system, I remained unaware. I just thought I was upset, or maybe it was nerves; they used to tell me, "You're the nervous type," or my favorite— "It's all in your head."

In my teens, I developed what was labeled as a "weak area" in my teeth and gums. I endured many painful and probably unhelpful dental procedures until my late twenties, when I began to realize my dental issues had meaning—they were messages.

My First Renaissance Teacher

In my late twenties, I experienced a crisis with my teeth and gums and was told by several dental specialists that I would probably lose all of my teeth. I had full-mouth periodontal surgery, which seemed to make things worse. The dentists all told me that I was losing bone in my jaws, and they did not know why. I was in pain, afraid, and confused about what to do.

The turning point for me—a day that forever changed the way I handled my life and my health—took place in the office of a well-known periodontist. He was extremely authoritative. After briefly examining me, he announced that one of my teeth was dead and would fall out soon, so we should just extract it. I disagreed, saying I knew it was a bit shaky, but it was alive. He produced something that looked like a small electric cattle prod and approached my tooth with it, saying, "Here, I'll show you it's dead." I stopped him immediately, took my little paper bib off, and said, "Excuse me, Doctor, but I cannot let you proceed. I am leaving." I jumped down out of the chair as he stood there stunned. I doubt that anyone had ever done this to him.

Feeling a rush of personal power, I breezed out past the office staff, telling them to "just send me a bill," and rushed out onto the busy city street. I took a few deep breaths and laughed out loud with joy at having freed myself. Then I became almost paralyzed with fear. Now what? I made a big declaration up in that office, but who would help me now? I could not go back, though, and I prayed for assistance. Help came in the form of a humble but genius-level professional who was a teacher, a healer, and a true Renaissance man.

A friend of mine referred me to this teacher. He was a dentist she had known for many years, and whom her children loved so much they had a nickname for him. Because he often laughed and made them laugh (not cry), they lovingly called him Dr. Ho Ho. Dr. H was an alternative practitioner of dentistry in the late 1970s when such people were almost non-existent.

There is no proper way to thank Dr. H, nor is there a real way to measure the depth and breadth of the impact he had on my life. A student of Linus Pauling, he was also a student of chemistry, energy, sports medicine, and so much more. He was surely not just a dentist. He was a Renaissance Man. He was also an immigrant to the United States. Even though he had been in our country for many years, Ho Ho retained just a bit of an accent and his own fresh way of using English.

When I first met the doctor, I had been told by several dentists that I would lose my teeth because I was losing bone around the roots, despite (or because of) tons of periodontal work and even an early attempt at a bone graft. Dr. H listened to my story, then smiled and asked, "Well, how you think we're gonna put the bone back in there?" Startled, I replied, "I thought that was what you were going to tell me!" He began laughing and tilted his head back, clapping his hands together. I knew then that this would be a much different adventure than I ever imagined.

Week after week, I would go to Dr. H's office and we would talk. He did nothing invasive to my teeth. What he did was teach me new ways of caring for my teeth and caring for myself. I learned a new way of thinking and being that launched my renaissance. I learned about vitamins, minerals, exercise, energy meridians, my muscular-skeletal system, and my body chemistry. I learned where to get the things I needed to care for myself, and how to use nutrition, exercise, breathing, massage, and meditation to help myself along the path.

I realized that I was commanding my health, at conscious *and* subconscious levels.

I was continuously amazed at the revelations on how easy and straightforward my body's own wisdom really was. For example, I participated in the workout craze of the 1980s and became an avid student of dance aerobics. I was working out a lot and noticed that the lateral side of my right foot was becoming more and more painful and swollen. One day, the pain was so great that I could not walk, so I hobbled to the nearest ER, where I sat for hours. They gave me a pain medication and sent me home with crutches. Instead of getting better, I got worse. An adverse reaction to the drug increased my swelling, and by Monday, I was miserable. I called Dr. H and he told me to come right in.

I sat teary-eyed in the dental chair there for him to see my foot. Now I had really gone off the edge—seeing a dentist for my foot! He came in and lovingly looked at my sad face. "Do not worry," he said. "Please, can you pull up your pant leg?" I did this, and he immediately made contact with a painful knot in my right calf that sent nerve pain right down into the affected spot on the foot. As he massaged, the pain subsided, until finally both calf and foot were only slightly sore. "What did you do? How did that work so fast?" I exclaimed. I had just discovered muscular trigger points.

Dr. H looked at me with such compassion, and also mirth, as he said, "You can always call me when something like this happens.

You see, they did not know how to help you in that ER; it's not their fault. You are like a Jaguar sports car; at the ER, they only have a Chevy manual. This won't work on you, see?" The Chevy manual at the ER did not have Ho Ho's troubleshooting kit—that's for sure. Doctor H showed me that it was possible to cast a vastly wider diagnostic net and capture an expanded view of health and healing that could yield a much more focused and lasting result.

At one point in my experience with Dr. H, I became vegetarian, as we revised my diet to create more optimal body chemistry. This dietary change seemed to be working, but after several months, I began to get cravings for hamburgers. It was all I could do to keep my car on the road when passing a burger place. I finally had to admit this and ask for guidance. He laughed when I told him, saying, "Oh, that's okay. Meat is your ancestral diet. Every once in a while, you must have bite of passing cow!" From then on, I have allowed myself those yummy bites and passed this lighthearted wisdom on to others.

Another valuable and very useful lesson I learned from Dr. H: taking nutritional supplements to improve health is fine, but there is much more to it. I was doing everything I could to reverse bone loss—taking all sorts of supplements, especially calcium and other minerals, yet I still had problems. Frustrated, I asked Dr. H why he thought I was losing bone in my jaws if I was taking all the "right" supplements. He responded: "Question not intake; question *absorption*."

I learned that one-size-fits-all does not work for most prescriptions—whether they be foods, vitamin, mineral or herbal supplements, medications, or even exercises. My body's specific needs had to be determined first. But how?

Suddenly, a light went on. I realized that I could use applied kinesiology or AK.[4] Learning and using AK enabled me to "test before I ingest" any food or supplement to make sure my body needed it and that it could be absorbed. I encourage all my clients and friends to find a reliable method of testing for themselves so they need not rely on the many experts out there to determine their unique nutritional or other health needs.

Working with Dr. H was my first experience with a real-life master. He gently facilitated my awakening, nudging me along by provoking ideas and thought until I made discoveries. I learned to think differently which caused me to become aware of the sturdy set of beliefs and associated judgments and actions that had governed my life. I began to question everything. All those things I previously knew as right or wrong became less clear, including what constituted health. I started to realize that the basis for true health was so much deeper and broader than the physical body. Health was a vast existential terrain, and I was now officially an explorer.

One of my most memorable revelations about people's different existential states came in a conversation where I was complaining to Dr. H that my aunt was never happy. Nothing seems to help or cheer her. She complains continuously. She cannot make decisions. She is a mess! What can we do? He calmly said to me, "Why do you think she is unhappy? Maybe you are unhappy with her behavior, but she may be just fine! For some people, pain and suffering is just their preferred way to live, so to them it's normal. For them, it may be a kind of happiness." When he said this, something suddenly clicked and shifted my awareness of others forever.

I realized that while there was a growing population beginning to make their own renaissance discoveries, most people still lived in the old world. There were many parallel worlds of awareness and belief acting as diverse existential "zip codes." These zip codes were invisible, of course, but there were as many of them as there were possible beliefs, cultures or individuals. I learned that it was okay for me to live in my current zip code and visit others, just like I would if I went to another neighborhood or city to see a friend. I did not have to reside there. Further, I was always free to move into a new zip code. This revelation gave me freedom – as long as I could remember that I was not stuck in any prescribed version of reality, I was free to navigate my own exciting journey.

My experience with Dr. H began my renaissance, as I discovered a new world of health and new ways of perceiving life itself. The experience launched my lifelong passion and study of alternative healthcare. I began to understand that my body was a greater miracle than any of us had been told. I learned to look beyond a physical symptom to understand what might be causing any dis-ease. I also realized more and more that my body really did obey my commands—known or unknown, helpful or harmful—and that truly knowing what sub-conscious or unconscious commands I might be giving was the key to health.

The new world of alternative health offered me many more options to care for myself.

I had to learn how to judge when to address a symptom with allopathic medicine and when I could afford to wait a bit and give the new ways a try. In the 1980s, there was not much help here, and the Internet connections we rely on today were not yet there. Awareness was more complicated than I imagined.

CHALLENGES OF EXPANDED HEALTHCARE

Especially now, properly caring for our body/minds represents one of our most critical challenges. I deal with my physical issues first by reassessing them holistically as messages from my body/mind interface. Then I seek professional assistance from both alternative and allopathic medicine as appropriate. Making these decisions has taught me a lot about my own fears and beliefs about my body, and trusting my own innate wisdom.

Prevailing beliefs are extremely powerful. At least in the United States, the collective consciousness defines our physical well-being not by degrees of health but by the absence or presence of disease. Just as we do not think of being human as a powerful asset, we do not think of ourselves as healthy. We are not trained to think of our bodies as powerful systems that are working continuously to create and maintain vitality and health. We learn the opposite—that our bodies are flawed and vulnerable. Because of this, we learn to be on a constant lookout for problems, and we are programmed to look for specific issues at specific ages. Loaded with these negative beliefs and programmed triggers, we struggle to maintain health throughout a lifetime. The renaissance challenges us to reprogram ourselves and literally re-member our power. If we take up this challenge, I think our renaissance could be quite dramatic.

Our definition of holistic healthcare expands with each new discovery about ourselves.

As we become more aware of our expansive suite of body/mind features, we realize how many more ways we can care for ourselves. Mainstream culture is catching up. People are discovering new options, so the market is demanding expanded and alternative healthcare approaches. This expansion of awareness can become a market driver for change in mainstream health systems and enhancements in health education.

This renaissance trend is already catching on, as one can see from articles in popular magazines on the wonders of "alternative practices." Since I have been writing this book, people who know me are always giving me articles or telling me about places they have heard "about the kind of stuff you do." Recently, my hairdresser pointed me to an article in a magazine which described the author's (and her husband's) gratifying results with a practitioner who used applied kinesiology techniques to target and release long-standing emotional dis-ease.[5]

Another article in the same magazine dealt with an author's discovery of Eastern-based energy medicine, including chakras, meridians, and the larger field of energy, consciousness, and frequency. She quotes an interviewee as saying, "The world is an energy soup. Western doctors have neither the tools nor the training to understand the phenomena."[6] While I have found many Western medicine doctors to be quite enlightened, the medical field still seems largely disconnected when it comes to holistic healthcare. I see significance in the fact that we often still label ancient, valid medical systems as "alternative" or "complementary." We thus perpetuate a binary medical model which gives clear priority to our relatively new allopathic system.

The two essays I cite are examples of a trend that one can see in almost any self-help journal or magazine. The fact that such articles are available in popular media is fantastic news, but the news can take some time to produce observable change in everyday life. In fact, when someone calls my attention to this sort of information, it is always presented as non-mainstream or marginal. Friends and colleagues happily produce these references as if to help me support "that stuff you do." At present, we have to understand that we live in at least two worlds of healthcare, with quite different perceptions about our health and how to care for it.

It can be frightening to live between these two worlds of healthcare. Having been raised in the consensus medical model and brought up to have pretty much automatic medical responses to all health issues, I have to be very conscious and calm whenever I have a health issue. I must always be aware of my options and maintain the balance I believe will create the best outcomes, given my current knowledge.

Since embarking on my own renaissance, I have had many scary experiences, often in the middle of the night by myself, trying to decide what to do about a health problem. I emphasize that I see myself as a kind of human laboratory for my own renaissance, so even if I am afraid, I explore my own frontier within what I believe to be safe parameters. I do not advise that anyone else do what I have done. I use my experience to explain and demonstrate what I have found to be possible for me.

My experience has taught me that sometimes very severe and frightening symptoms can be my body interface sending messages that may not require or be successfully addressed by conventional medical means. I have taken numerous trips to the emergency room that turned up nothing but a big bill, long waits, and lots of bruising. I will still go if I think it is right. I will call 911! But I usually try some alternative steps first. I am blessed to know several talented alternative health professionals who either stay up late or live in time zones hours behind mine.

For example, while writing this book, I experienced some extreme physical symptoms in areas of my body that had historically challenged me. This continuing process lets me know I am pushing my own limits, challenging aspects of my fear firewall. My body signals what she perceives as danger using her own unique signature messages, often through my teeth and gums. In addition, writing this book was a cathartic act, resulting in a cleansing or detoxification on many levels and dramatically affecting my lymphatic system.

One night, I experienced a huge issue. Of course, it was a weekend night. One side of my mouth, gums, teeth, face, eyes, sinus, and the whole lymphatic drainage system on that side of my head was painful, inflamed, and swollen. My gums were bleeding, and some teeth were so sore I could not bite down on them. I texted a friend who practices distance healing using a modality called NeuroModulation Technique, or NMT, and asked if she could do a session for me.[7]

I did not know when my friend would do during the session, but about an hour after calling her, I felt the whole side of my head draining, and the pain just left. Swelling and bleeding subsided; teeth were no longer sore. I texted my friend to tell her, and she was extremely pleased. She told me the exact time she had done the session, which was just when I felt the relief, and she sent me the results. Briefly, she had cleared my field of consciousness and emotional issues. Although the lymphatic system in my head was dramatically congested, the causal agent was not microbial. It was rather a suite of consciousness phenomena—all invisible.

Although infection was present in my mouth, it was not the priority for treatment that night. It was not causal. I have come to believe that many microbial issues—what we think of infections—often occur at sites in the body weakened by holding emotional or consciousness "issues in the tissues." Further, many more medical professionals now accept the links of various body areas to acupuncture meridians and their associated organs. In the case of teeth, charts are readily available on the Internet that show which teeth correspond to which organs and meridians. Trouble in an associated organ or meridian can mean difficulty in the associated teeth.

Additionally, the mouth itself has an emotional and consciousness aspect—it is the portal through which we nourish ourselves and from which we speak our truth. For me, speaking my truth, or writing it, always caused issues in my mouth. For example, I met Dr. Ho Ho as I was finishing my Ph.D. and writing my dissertation—I was in incredible dental distress. During the creation of *Human Renaissance,* I have had numerous dental issues, like the one described above. The book represented not only a major project but also a life work and a declaration of my position—some scary issues.

My body's dental alarm signals always got louder when I was taking the next step into a new world—a new career or endeavor—outside my familiar world. I learned that the consciousness of teeth represents decision-making, trusting and taking action to implement decisions. Our common phrase, "bit off more than you could chew," speaks to our underlying belief that if one goes beyond some point of perceived capability, one will be unable to handle or "chew" it. My dental issues were possible messages to me regarding my mistrust of my own decisions and feeling that I had taken on too much.

After years of such experiences, I have begun to trust my message systems. So when I get symptoms, I first consult my consciousness, energy systems, emotions, and so on before I jump to a physical resolution. For me, this course of action has no downside risk, as it is completely non-invasive and can do no harm. Further, it works to help me unburden myself of issues I can deal with, so that my need for intervention decreases as my overall health increases. When I do determine there is a priority for a medical intervention, it usually has great results because I did a lot of preparation.

One important challenge for me in the world of alternative healthcare was learning to deal with my own expectations regarding how the healing process works. Even though I now realize that health is not a static state, and that healing is a process with many stages and layers, I grew up at the start of the instant fix medical generation in the 1950s and '60s. If it hurts or is inflamed, you go put something on it, get a shot, take a pill, or have the thing cut out and you are instantly fixed. Not so in the alternative world, where the body truly does the healing in its own way, which can be instant, but often is a process that may be difficult, addressing underlying causes rather than symptoms. No matter how much I know, I still find myself impatient with the process of natural healing, especially if my symptoms get worse before I get better.

I am still frustrated that along the path to great health, I can look and feel awful. Once I began to clear out toxic chemicals, metals, emotional and consciousness toxins, and other harmful imbalances, I found I often felt and looked really tired and sick. We have all heard of the term "healing crisis," also called a Herxheimer reaction, and we know at some level that something can feel worse as it is on its way to clearing. A fever breaking is a common example of this. Nevertheless, I am often surprised at the way my body will choose to re-form or heal, and disappointed that it involves discomfort and time.

I have learned that even really good health is more a journey than a destination. Although one can certainly feel 100 percent healthy at times, more than likely one cycles through various states of 100 percent health, since most of us must do quite a bit of clearing to create conditions for vibrant, natural health.

A senior BodyTalk practitioner and instructor employs an excellent analogy to help explain the process of attaining health. She likens all the issues a person may accumulate over the years to a stack of plates.[8] Year after year, the stack gets higher, an injury here, a toxin there, a trauma, and so on. By the time the client presents with symptoms, the stack can be quite tall. Somewhere down the stack, there might be that one magic causal plate. But we cannot necessarily know that. We have to work our way there with the body's permission and guidance, removing the most appropriate plates at the right times.

We can build new healthcare models based on health, not disease.

Expanded healthcare options take some time to incorporate, but it is worth the adjustment. My father taught me a great lesson about decision-making. When I was having trouble deciding what part-time job to take and getting upset, he said, "Well, kid, at least you have a decision to get upset over. If you had no options, it would sure make the decision easy. Be grateful for your trouble." I am grateful for all our current health options, and I believe that if we cooperate, people can have enough information to make optimal choices for themselves. Ultimately, we can live in a world where health, not disease, governs the process and experience of health-care.

5
Emotional Power: Feeling Our Way

All honest emotions are positive emotions.

Candace Pert, *Molecules of Emotion*

Our rich emotional system provides us with a power resource that constitutes a new world in itself. Emotions function as a key driver in our lives, yet we are almost completely untrained in their use, or in the many ways they can be abused or manipulated.

In fact, our cultural and educational systems often neglect or demonize this resource. We are trained to experience many of our core emotions as disruptive antagonists of a civilized life. Emotions we label as negative, like anger or fear, are pretty much banned from our public life, unless we are out of control. Although positive emotions, like joy or passion, can be acceptable, we learn that they must be controlled in contexts like the workplace, where we spend most of our lives.

Even those of us who would say we know better are programmed by potent belief systems that an ideal life should be free of emotional disturbances. Many people fear strong emotion of any kind. We know instinctively that emotions are powerful, and because we have no good training in managing them, we fear we cannot control them if they break out into our nice neat lives. Thus, we set up an ambivalent, almost adversarial relationship with this core feature of ourselves.

To stay safe and in control, we often prefer to experience strong emotions vicariously or express them in a context that is set off from our regular life. The many ways we do this include artistic or sporting activities and events, all genres of novels, movies or TV programs that evoke strong emotions: humor, action, horror, romance, erotica or pornography, and many more. It is OK for us to express emotion when playing a sport, for example, or when playing an instrument. These are good ways to learn to use emotions, but one wonders how we might integrate our power more fully to help us throughout life.

Emotion also sells. We buy products that use strong emotional messages. We love to follow TV series that have characters with strong emotional appeal. We crave stories about people's emotional lives. We want details. We allow ourselves to react to these reflections of our own emotional power, but we deny or misunderstand how to proactively use that power in everyday life. And the more stressful our lives get, the greater the market becomes for strong emotion in formats other than our everyday life.

Our emotional system operates 24/7, causing continuous change in our bodies.

Our emotions carry a charge or frequency that we now know alters us at cellular levels. Candace Pert's groundbreaking work, *Molecules of Emotion* (1997), describes in detail her scientific study and proofs that emotions and our biochemistry are one, and that all changes in our emotional state create changes at a cellular level.[9]

Over fifteen years ago, Pert wrote: "The tendency to ignore our emotions is *oldthink,* a remnant of the still reigning paradigm that keeps us focused on the material level of health, the physicality of it. But the emotions are a key element in self-care because they allow us to enter into the bodymind's conversation. By getting in touch with our emotions, both by listening to them and by directing them through the psychosomatic network, we gain access to the healing wisdom that is everyone's natural biological right."[10]

Unfortunately, the "oldthink" that Pert decries remains the norm today. In our increasingly stressful world, the results are proportionately devastating. Emotions are power that we can use to shift and create our reality, for better or for worse. The charge of emotion can become lodged in our body and create serious dis-ease. Beginning with early mainstream works like that of Norman Cousins' *Anatomy of an Illness*,[11] we have a huge body of proof that healing and health result when we harness this power.

To understand more about our rich emotional toolkit, I also recommend Karla McLaren's book, *The Language of Emotions: What Your Feelings Are Trying to Tell You* (2010). She sums up our dilemma when she states:

> We've neatly sewn up our emotions, and in so doing, we've sewn ourselves right into a straightjacket. Anyone who feels anything other than the light, fresh-scented emotions is, by association, bad. This simplistic good/bad system imprisons so many of us: we who are angry, we who are grieving, we who are fearful, we who feel shame—many of us with legitimate emotional issues are pushed out of the way to make room for the perky and the superficial.[12]

As McLaren and others show, the rich resource of our emotions provides us with an effective and efficient message interface. We just need to learn how to translate our own meaning to understand what we are feeling and why. My experience taught me that I often cried or laughed out loud when something very important was happening and warranted my full attention. This signal was perfect but a completely incorrect behavior based on what I was taught. Once I trusted these signals as messengers, I became more able to use my emotional resource. I learned by experiencing and exploring my own body/mind reactions.

I experienced a very clear demonstration of my emotional body interface when I decided to quit my job as a professor and launch my own business. As I got ready to quit my job, I experienced lots of messaging I was not trained to understand. Here I was, choosing to abandon the tenure-track position that my parents, friends, and colleagues expected of me. For years, this type of job had been my dream, but when I got to the point of fulfilling this dream, it was not correct for me. It felt all wrong and I knew I had to do something else. Leaving the academic world for the unknown world of business was a radical shift, a frightening new voyage of discovery.

Luckily, I had a holistic primary care physician who was teaching me to be more aware of my systems and their messages. My doctor was not surprised when I told her about the heart palpitations and chest pain. She sent me directly to a cardiologist for examination and testing. She explained, "Clare, understand that your heart literally sits in the middle between your head and your gut, and mediates between these two. When there is such dissonance, as you have now in this decision, you can experience dis-ease in the system. The heart is uncomfortable, but we need to make sure she is healthy. That's first."[13]

At the cardiologist, I went through all the tests: EKG, ultrasound, and stress test. The doctor then took me into his office and said, "Clare, you are fine. Your heart is very strong." I sighed. "Now," he continued, "I never discount symptoms, and you have had symptoms. I have seen too many beautiful eyes close for the last time because someone didn't follow up on a symptom." (I have loved this man forever because he said this.) "However," he continued, "I do not think your symptoms are caused by heart disease of any physical kind. You know what I think?" I replied no. "I think that Little Clare is scared; that sweet little girl inside of you is afraid."

Upon hearing that, I burst into sobs, exclaiming between large blows of my nose, "I made a big mistake quitting my job. Now I'll be broke. I don't want to have to work at some fast food place flipping burgers!" The doctor waited until the sobs subsided, and then looked lovingly at me and said, "Don't worry, dear Clare, I do not think they'd hire you at those places anyway—you're overqualified!" We both laughed.[14]

After being assured that I was physically sound, my heart settled down. I had made my decision and felt more secure that it was correct. My fears and emotional dis-ease had been acknowledged and calmed. I was just starting to understand the deep level of emotional programming able to influence the health of my whole body system.

To develop the ability to receive emotional messages, I had to learn how to listen to myself.

Many of the alarm messages I have received from my body completely resolved when I let my body know I was listening. Emotions held in particular places in my body could cause intense distress, but could be gone almost like magic if the triggering emotional cause was released or resolved. I was learning about "issues in the tissues."

In addition to coding emotional issues as somatic dis-ease or discomfort, my body sent messages coded as purely emotional responses to physical (non-sexual) touch. I had no training in how to decode these messages either, so at first they were surprising and sometimes embarrassingly intense. Through experiencing different types of bodywork, I learned that even very light touch on my body could cause intense emotional reactions.

Although I had been doing regular exercise for many years, except for Dr. Ho Ho, no one had really introduced me to the many ways my body actually worked. Then one day, a woman in an exercise class turned to me and asked, "Who does your bodywork?" I was embarrassed to tell her not only that I did not have anyone, but also that I really didn't know what she meant. She was very surprised and said that as a dancer, she would not have been able to do anything without having professionals work with her body. She gave me some contacts, and I was on my way to new discoveries about the emotional and consciousness components of my body.

Starting with my colleague's referrals, I began to experience various types of bodywork, such as deep tissue massage, myofascial release, Feldenkrais, craniosacral therapy, and naprapathy.[15] In many of these treatments, I found myself suddenly sobbing, laughing, or somehow emoting like crazy. At first, I was embarrassed, but each therapist assured me that this type of release was normal and essential to the treatments. I came to look forward to it as I better understood that my body was holding onto various "charges" based on emotional content. Just experiencing the emotions was enough. There was no need to explain or understand them in an analytical way. Often, some memory would accompany the emotional release, like a short video clip from my childhood—a scene or memory of an event or interaction, which would quickly pass by. All of this was new to me.

Through bodywork, I could access emotional content and release issues that were causing dis-ease. In the process, I became not only more balanced, but also felt freer at all levels. This feeling of the freedom to BE, to feel however I was feeling at any time, has been a very important part of my renaissance, and it was an emotional learning. As I visited more alternative practitioners, I was constantly amazed at the healing power of a healthcare environment where I felt free from the judgment or evaluation. I was free to allow my body/mind to express whatever came up.

One belief I discovered I had was that if I became sick or had a problem, I was somehow weak or incorrect, or even bad. This caused a shameful feeling, so it affected my experience of being seen by a doctor. Being "examined" often felt more like an Inquisition to find wrong-doing than it did like an exercise in health. I often wonder if the nervous reaction called "white coat syndrome" is based on this underlying program of shame and guilt about clinical examination or judgment more than it is anxiety about treatment or outcome. Discovering that a healing environment could be safe was really liberating. I was learning not just the meaning, but the feeling of compassion and unconditional caring or love. Most importantly, I was learning that I could feel that way toward myself.

I was slowly exposing a huge belief system around not feeling well. I grew up with the belief that the good, responsible person always presents a positive face to the world, whether they feel good or not. Because of this, I felt ashamed about feeling unwell. Our educational and work cultures reinforce feelings of shame and discomfort around health issues. The workplace tracks employee sick days carefully, only paying for a specific number of days per year. Many organizations allow employees to accumulate unused sick days and take them as additional pay, so the organization rewards people for NOT ever taking days off, even if they should. The result is that we have a nation of people operating sub-optimally at work so they can accumulate more money.

In the United States, we are prepared for this system in elementary and secondary school, where absences are tracked and students made to present "excuses" (interesting choice of words) for sick days or any absence. My mother used to *make sure* I was sick if I wanted to stay home one day, so my body probably learned to put on a good show. One young professional I spoke to recently said that she opted out of corporate life because she hated the thought "that you couldn't even feel sick without feeling worse because you had to call in sick!" All these examples highlight the importance of enhanced awareness regarding the emotional component of our being and our health, and the ways our culture trains us to value or de-value that crucial part of ourselves.

Emotions can be seen as the creative force or "juice" of life.

The immense creative power of emotions is not a topic we learn much about, yet we know about it instinctively—Bob's Law! When I began to study the ancient art of manifestation I learned that although all creation begins with an idea, emotion supplies the power or fire that births it into the world. From ancient times, people have known emotion as the fire of creation, yet it is not taught to us as a creative tool, except possibly in artistic activities—poetry, music, dance, acting, or graphic arts. Nevertheless, since emotion is functioning all the time as a major human creative force, it pays to take stock of how it is creating things in our daily lives.

In my work as a consultant, I have participated in hundreds of engagements to resolve interpersonal issues that were based on emotional reactions to behavior or judgments about behavior. Our invisible masters—our beliefs—derive much of their force from emotion. The power of deep belief, as we know, can create miracles or tragedies, but it definitely creates. Emotions function brilliantly whether they are what we think of as positive or negative, and they all have power we can understand.

We know that the energy we call love includes a constellation of emotions, and carries enormous positive power. Love in the fullest sense is probably the highest, most effective healing frequency. Every hurt child feels better when held by a loving parent, or having a boo-boo kissed to make the pain go away. The energy or frequency of love has been studied and data has been collected that prove the positive efficacy of this power we all possess.[16] Joy, peace, and happiness all carry powerful health-giving frequencies, and thus are used in healing meditations, prayers, and affirmations.

It is easy to comprehend the positive creative power of emotions that we consider to be positive, like love or joy or happiness, but what about the ones we consider negative? Often, as I learned in bodywork sessions, just feeling and releasing a negative or disturbing emotional charge creates better health. But I have also found that using negative emotional power proactively can help me deal better with life. For example, while fear may block me sometimes, it is also useful as an emotion of survival. Awareness of fear and its causes is crucial to staying healthy and productive, because so many aspects of daily life trigger this emotion. Chapter 10 in Part Three deals with fear exclusively.

Anger is a great motivator. Just listen to one of the many television reality show "drill sergeants" shouting angry commands to the harried participants to spur them to action. Or we can think of the traditional "Socratic method" teacher who berates and bullies the students until they fight back with improved, more precise responses. Also, we often get ourselves past a place in life or work where we are stuck by just "blasting" out, using anger as our power pack. It works! As long as we "command the force" of anger, we are healthy. It is when it sneaks up in negative ways toward others or ourselves that it becomes a danger. Positive anger seems to be all about pushing past blocks to manifest our creations. With so many blocks in our way today, and so many people frustrated and unable to create a decent life, do we wonder why there seems to be rampant anger?

Sadness can be challenging because it is so difficult for others to know how to handle this strong emotion in the worlds of polite society or work. We do not receive good training in just being there for someone who is sad; there really is nothing to do. Sadness definitely stops the action of the one feeling it, and anyone else who is around. This power to stop the activity has the positive effect of forcing reflection. As long as the reflection does not become excessive, it can help us to identify and acknowledge our feelings. The BodyTalk system taught me that sadness was the "flip side" of joy, so one positive outcome of sadness for me is that I can use the time to reflect on what the missing joy might be, and rekindle that positive, life-giving feeling.

Grief seems to work in a similar way to sadness, but with much more active force. In the last decade, I experienced grief in what seemed to be a never-ending series of family deaths over a six-year period. Grief for me was a primal cleansing and opening at levels I did not know I had. Like most people, I experienced grief not just as a constant underlying sadness but also as unpredictable waves of uncontrolled sobbing, shaking, and feelings of absolute desolation. Working through this period, using all of the modalities I could, allowed me to clear myself as I never had before, like a true re-birth.

The wondrous payoff of grief for me was the way it opened my heart. Much is written about the benefits of surrender or of being cracked open and freed to love. All this seemed conceptually right to me, but I did not fully realize the meaning until my own difficult experience of losing loved ones and parents. My understanding of being human is more an emotional knowing that comes from my heart. My heart-brain was ultimately strengthened by processing this emotional content and by being honored as a center of wisdom.

A loving support network allowed me to benefit from an experience that may have caused damage if handled differently, or not addressed at all. I wonder how much heart dis-ease, surgery, and suffering we might avoid and what new levels of comfort and health we might achieve, if we knew better how to deal with our strong emotional experiences.

EXERCISE:

To explore emotional power and learn to use it better, we need to practice listening to our emotions. Here are some key steps I take to detect emotional issues, and begin to address them.

1. **Whenever you feel pushback** within yourself, which may present as mental, emotional, or physical discomfort, take a moment and **observe it.** Focus on that signal.
2. **Ask yourself what may be causing the discomfort and listen for an emotion.** Even if you cannot change what you are about to do (like go to work at a job you dislike), take a minute to listen to yourself.
3. If you are having trouble listening to yourself, **consider the many belief programs that might be in the way**. I find it easy just to jot down or speak a few of the "lessons" we were all taught that function to silence our inner voices or punish us for feeling something "unacceptable." Here are a few examples:

- Do not talk to yourself. Only crazy people do that.
- If you feel sad, tired, or anxious, you are weak. Weakness is not OK.
- Suck it up! There is nothing wrong with you. You have no discipline.
- You are imagining this; it is not real.

4. **Address any blocking beliefs by acknowledging them**. Ask them to just be at peace for a moment, to let go, so you can feel what your body is trying to tell you. This is much like "dropping the charges" against yourself. Then tune in to the signal you are getting and ask again for the emotion or message.
5. Once you think you understand what the emotional message is, **let your body/mind know that you HEAR it,** and that you will do whatever you can to make things better. I often get excellent results when I ask exactly what to do to resolve this feeling. The answer is often fairly simple.
6. **If you cannot resolve the issue immediately**, try telling yourself that you need to be OK right now and **make a date later on to revisit**. You can also make an appointment with a professional to get help facilitating a resolution. The main thing is that you let your body/mind know that you have love and compassion for this issue, even if you can't deal with it completely at this time.

There are many ways to address an emotional issue that pops up and gets in the way, but most involve the same first step – acknowledging and *not resisting* the emotion or emotions that we feel. On my journey I have experimented with lots of methods. I highly recommend the Emotional Freedom Technique or EFT, which uses tapping points on the body, eye movements, and language to release and shift the underlying causes of emotionally-based dis-ease.[17] EFT is easy to learn, requires no equipment or special space, and can be done almost anywhere. Even in a work situation, one can usually take a few moments to go to the rest room and tap (smile).

Discovering the new worlds of our emotions is a continuous journey and can be fun. It certainly deepens our understanding of all people and ourselves. Most importantly, it helps us to actually use this immense creative resource.

6
Mind and Super-Mind: Limitless Resources

The Mind is its own place, and in itself
Can make a Heav'n of Hell, a Hell of Heav'n.

John Milton, *Paradise Lost*

As Milton's fallen angel makes clear in *Paradise Lost*, the invisible "place" of the mind functions as an active force that can create worlds. Our mind, on all levels, is one of our most significant renaissance tools. We can re-learn the ways our mind actually works—how we receive, process, and create the data of our lives. We are taught to believe that our mind must be disciplined and trained in a very left-brained way—to think logically, process data using categories and protocols and Harvard outlines. Early on, many of us experience dissonance when other non-linear features within our whole mind or consciousness want to be recognized. We can discover the new worlds of our own minds.

Most of us have at least one experience that demonstrates the function of our higher consciousness, a supra-mental component that receives and processes information even if we are not in our body. I call this the super-mind. I learned about my super-mind in a near-fatal car accident.

It was early December and snowing hard as I drove toward Cleveland to join a college friend for a vacation trip. As night fell, I encountered a snowstorm in a well-known snow belt area. The stream of snow in the headlights was steady and mesmerizing, and I chewed gum and sang to stay alert. Although I was an experienced snow driver, I was also tired. I kept my speed down, but the car ahead of me was weaving across the lanes and slowing down rapidly; I could not seem to avoid hitting him in the rear. In an effort to miss him, I panicked and applied the brakes. The brakes locked up, and the car began skidding out of control—right into and across a wide grassy median and into the busy lanes of traffic moving in the opposite direction.

As this was happening, I left my body for the first time. Suddenly, I could see myself in the driver's seat, see the grimace on my face, and hear my screams and the squealing of the car. But I was viewing this awful scene from about four feet above the car itself, looking through the roof like it was not there. I remember thinking, *How awful for that poor girl—look how terrified she is.* I watched in sadness, until I realized it was me! At just about that time, my perspective was instantly shifted. With something that felt like a thud, I was suddenly looking out of my own body's eyes again—staring into the blinding headlights of a semi truck that had stopped inches from my driver's side door.

The car was a total loss, but I had only whiplash. Miraculously, no one else was injured. Although I had not yet begun to study the phenomenon of consciousness, I experienced it dramatically: I learned that day that not only was it possible for my consciousness to separate from my physical body, but that if it was necessary because of an impending traumatic or painful death, it would happen automatically. My body/mind had more features than I knew. I possessed a component that was capable of removing my consciousness from my body if she decided the danger was too great. In addition to helping me be less afraid of death, the discovery of this powerful ability forever expanded how I thought about myself. It made me feel safer and more confident.

A renaissance person develops an expanded mind, creating a consciousness toolkit.

The challenge, as with most of our renaissance abilities, is that we are not trained to understand or trust these options as real or part of our everyday lives. When the mental body interface shows us data through more right-brain or intuitive channels, we often doubt it or discount it altogether. When faced with a demonstration of the super-mind, as with my car accident, we often discount it as our imagination, or some extraordinary occurrence. We are taught that super-natural can't be natural. But what if it is?

By now, we can pretty much agree that our mind is not the same as our brain, although that relationship between thinking and the processes of our brain is crucial.[18] But our mind is largely a consciousness phenomenon. From Plato to current scholars, spiritual teachers, and scientists, the growing body of literature supports this. We now know that our whole being has and IS consciousness. We are consciousness beings with systems functioning at all levels: physical, emotional, mental, and spiritual or super-mental.

Signals from our mind and super-mind most often come to us in the invisible formats we call thoughts or ideas. We have been taught to categorize qualities of thought in a binary way, perhaps reflective of the overall dualism of our consensus reality—we define thinking as either left-brain or right-brain, indicating a qualitative, not a physiological, difference. The left-brain function for us is a much more linear process, usually involving what we call logic, the processing of objective data and ideas according to some pre-approved sequential protocol. We also call this left-brain quality "rational."

The right-brain function has a non-linear quality and is considered more intuitive, processing data that may not be strictly factual or visible. This function also draws conclusions without a pre-approved sequential process, moving randomly or laterally, solving problems in new ways. We call this right-brain function "intuitive." This leaping, non-rational component can also be viewed as the software that allows us access to areas of the universal sea of consciousness that our belief system has placed outside normal thinking parameters and called extra-ordinary or para-normal. Such phenomena are often called spiritual; they may also be termed super-mental.

Increasingly, we realize that we possess both left and right-brain capabilities, and can use them together holistically to achieve renaissance results. We need our whole mind! Our challenge is that our right-brain function has not been honored in consensus reality as a valid processor, so we are not trained to use this huge functional area of our operating system.

Being able to access and use more of our whole mind allows us to discover new worlds.

Without the ability to access and use our whole mind, we cannot do what Einstein advised: discover new solutions to our existing problems. Throughout my exploration, I have been fortunate enough to receive support and teaching in using and trusting my right-brain functions and integrating them into a sort of whole mind. Like anything else, education in these crucial body/mind skills requires both conceptual and behavioral learning. Curricula for such learning must be made available to real, regular people if we are to lead large-scale change.

I found that re-discovering the expansive capabilities of my mind interface was often very challenging and frightening. When my right brain or intuitive mind began to send messages, I got a corresponding set of alarm messages from my left brain or logical mind. These logical messages told me I was imagining things, that the intuitive information was wrong, imaginary, or fake. At first, I dealt with this by overriding the alarm programs by sheer will even though I was afraid. As I began to trust the information more, I dared to tell someone else about it, which was a big step. One of my early teachers advised me to just go with it, and remember the old saying, "Fake it till you make it." He assured me that once I had successes and became more adept at recognizing reliable information, I would be fine. That was true.

I learned a lot about my intuitive message system as I began working with people to clear their chakras. I enjoyed the work and used what I had learned in Eden Energy Medicine and from studying the work of Barbara Brennan. I swept and cleared, and I got messages. When they first began to come, they were a bit fuzzy. As I began to trust my ability to receive data, the messages got quite clear. Although I am not primarily a visual person, when I work with chakras I often get very vivid scenes from someone's life. Of course, at first it felt risky to tell the client what I saw, especially because many of the scenes were unpleasant or even violent. After all, they were coming up to be cleared.

My alternative teachers were always supportive and encouraged my new discoveries, and if I was practicing in a workshop, I was with like-minded folks. However, when it was just me with a client on my table, I felt pretty vulnerable. It did not take long, though, until I knew I had to say something about what was going on. If the clients wanted to know what I was getting, I would tell them within reason. I found that when I used discretion in telling clients about messages that were revealed, their reaction was always positive.

One of the first times I decided to tell a client about the messages I received, the scene I saw was dramatic. I saw a fatal boating accident with crashing waves, and I actually felt like I was inside a drowning child. I had trouble breathing and felt panic. When I told the client, he cried and said that this had happened when he was very young, and he did almost die. The memory was asking to be released. I have now had this type of experience hundreds of times with clients. I am grateful for my clients' trust and the opportunity to help them access their own information, allowing me to act as a facilitator.

Because all of our invisible resources operate simultaneously, mental data may be experienced emotionally or physically or both, and signals may show up in all of what I am calling interface areas simultaneously. In a world where we have no standard or accepted guidelines for our own operations, learning to translate, interpret, and use the interface data presents us with challenges such as those I experienced.

7
Learning to Use Invisible Assets

The trouble with most people is that they have no invisible means of support.

Joseph Murphy,
The Power of Your Subconscious Mind

Our newly-discovered invisible assets can present challenges for which we may be unprepared. Even when we are already experiencing expanded awareness, we may still feel uncomfortable about the ways new information comes to us. For example, we might expect to receive data in a familiar message format—a written message, a picture, a voice saying words, a clear language, or representational direction. Although some people do receive data in familiar formats, others do not.

Just as some people see energy fields in very specific detail, some also receive super-mental messages visually. The messages may come as words, spoken or written, mathematical formulas, geometric shapes, or even very clear pictures. Messages may also use other sensory cues – sounds, smells, or somatic sensation. However, many of us rely primarily on what is often termed "felt sense" to understand consciousness-based data. This was my experience. From childhood I had "knowings" but I did not see or hear information, I just suddenly knew things and I *felt* them, and then I translated what I felt into a logical format, words and thoughts that would make sense in the outside world. Further, the feelings were not like emotions that we usually experience, although I might also feel a familiar emotion.

Because felt sense is complicated and difficult to trust, I want to describe my experience.

Felt sense cues may seem ambiguous, since they express meaning without words or visuals. It's almost like a pure frequency data transmission. Most people have received some sort of wordless message they later found to be true in the real everyday world. Many people I have met say they lost faith in the messages they received because they had no guidebook to understand their own internal communication system. To those whose primary access is feeling, I can tell you that it is often much more direct messaging than any of the other formats, and you should not give up. In time, you will develop the ability to use other sensory formats, but the felt sense may always be your primary access to the world of 99% invisible data.

Here is an example of how felt sense works for me when I am working with a client (or myself) and get a message. The first clue that I have a message comes through a combination of somatic and consciousness cues. My body usually presents some kind of cue as a sensation. Typically I get goose bumps, but it can also be burning or tingling in my hands, or a sort of high-pitched sound in my ears. I may also want to begin crying or laughing, or just suddenly feel a strong emotion of any kind—even anger. I may also feel dizzy or light-headed (look at that phrase). Often, I begin to yawn repeatedly.

Emotional and somatic cues tell me to pay attention, because I am receiving data.

When these things first began happening, of course, I was confused. Then I began to notice patterns I could use to know what was happening. I also got support and confirmation when others shared with me that they experienced these signals, too, and often the same ways I did.

Once I began to practice energetic balancing work with clients, I started to get surprising somatic signals in advance of a person even contacting me for a session. I would wake up in the morning with a tingling or even slight burning sensation or pulsing energy in the palms of my hands. Over time, I noticed a pattern: whenever I awoke with those sensations, someone would call me to work with them, or, during the day, a client would simply show up. This was my early warning system. I am now pretty used to it, and it still happens. Other practitioners have told me that they experience similar phenomena.

In addition to receiving overt signals from my body or emotions, I get felt-sense messages when working with a client. The data then comes in as a download which might be best compared to an epiphany. I instantly receive information regarding a situation, person, issue or problem. I have learned to speak out loud what I am getting, or write it down, so I can ask further questions or confirm if it is correct. I always laugh when I think of the various ways our current technology reflects our power for us in the many types of instant messaging we do every day. Our bodies knew how to send and receive insta-gram messages long before cell phones existed!

I was often overwhelmed and concerned when huge instant messages began flooding in, especially when a client was right there. My beliefs told me that the client was counting on me to be in control, and I was not always feeling that way. More importantly, success accessing and interpreting messages from a client's consciousness required *letting go* of my need to control the process or outcome. Over years of practice, I have learned that I am in control of this process, but not the way I was taught in traditional professional contexts.

My power relies on my ability to trust, not control, and to act as a facilitator instead of what I call the "answer man," the expert who answers or fixes your problems.

Our cultural beliefs about the power of experts and our role as an expert professional who advises clients, tends to leave the client out of the interaction. When I first began my consulting practice, I worried a lot about whether I knew everything needed to resolve a client's issues; I felt alone and unprepared. I felt pressure to fix instead of facilitate. I called my mentor one evening and confessed all this to him, to which he replied, "Why don't you just relax, Clare, and let the client play, too? You need to partner with the client! The client is why you're there."

In addition to learning how to partner with the client in the alternative healthcare setting, I also had to learn new ways to use my own mental processes. Receiving downloads in a session caused anxious moments because the information can come in very fast, and the data was often robust. When I first started getting the complex wordless downloads, I was afraid I wouldn't understand it fast enough, or be able to remember it long enough to get the whole picture. I was anxious about slowing down to ask questions—as if the material might disappear if I waited a second. Being a lifelong traditional student, I was trained that if I didn't write it down, I'd forget it, so I began to block when data came in so fast and in so many unfamiliar formats. After all, I was trained as a logical thinker, so part of me probably believed this was all imaginary, that it was not really possible.

It took a while—maybe a few years—to find ways to deal with this process. I learned how to remember and re-view the content of any download. I learned to slow down and expand my understanding of the information. Not only can I take time to write or dictate messages, I can also ask further questions about the content and meaning. The more questions I take time to ask, the more information I often get. I wonder if some version of this process allowed the early shaman to see Columbus's ships.

I learned to *let go* and allow my mind to *expand* into a new world of information.

I did this by asking lots of questions—yes, of myself—or so it seemed, because it was all going on in what felt like my mind. So I learned to talk to myself as an interface and listen carefully for answers. Often, the message I hear is wordless, more like a knowing, but I have learned to translate the knowing into words.

Luckily, there is often a phrase or word that keeps repeating, which acts as a clue, encouraging more questions. For example, I may hear a word or phrase repeating, but it is scrambled or muffled. I ask until I get more clarity. If working with a client, I can ask if they know what the word or phrase means, because they often do, but I have to be willing to tell them whatever crazy-sounding thing I am getting.

Once, a friend called me just as I was getting ready for work in the early morning. She was extremely distraught because her father had just passed away. I knew he had been seriously ill and his death was imminent. I had little experience trying to contact people who had passed, but she knew I had been learning about distance or remote healing, and that I believed in the ongoing life of the spirit. Because she was in tears and urgently begging me to contact him, I said I would try. I did my best to let go and asked to connect with him.

Suddenly, I felt very calm. Then I got goose bumps all over my body, and I heard a voice say, "I am all right, Puffy; do not worry. I love you." I silently and repeatedly asked the voice who Puffy was, and, receiving no answer, I decided to take the chance and just ask my friend. When I did, she began sobbing and said, "It's not Puffy, it's Puppy! He calls me Puppy!" The clue was provided so she would know it was her dad. He called her Puppy when she was little, and only he would say that. I learned that being willing to share even the most illogical information can have great results.

I am always learning about new information channels I possess but have not been trained to know or use. Using all the new aspects of my interface together has been like learning to drive a stick shift car. You think you will not be able to do all that at once, but you can! Even if I get a data download without somatic cues, I pay close attention to more subtle body cues and to my emotional state, because there is usually some really important information there.

My way of understanding and experiencing the world always relied primarily on somatic, emotional, or mental data, almost never on visual data. Our educational system, however, uses primarily visual method cues, and so even in many workshops intended to help develop the types of tools I am discussing, written or visual materials are still the primary learning medium. Also, during certain exercises, participants are often asked to *visualize* something – a part of a person, a scene, or event. After some years of feeling lost during these exercises, I learned to translate my own cues into a graphic or visual format.

Recently, I had a significant experience in translating data to a visual medium. I received a message during a meditation telling me there were specific symbols that would help me clear an issue by shifting the frequency. I was told that I was being shown the symbols, but I could not see them. Frustrated, I decided to just draw what I thought they looked like even though I did not *see* them. As I drew each line, I asked if this was right and found that the more I trusted my felt sense, the easier it was to draw. The whole exercise was very uncomfortable, as it was completely non-logical, and challenged just about every belief I still had left about what sane people do. The result was four symbols, somewhat resembling Reiki symbols. I have never seen these symbols anywhere else, but they worked for me.

Education, training, and practice are key to accessing and using any abilities. Although the training of one's internal interface is not widely available, it has been around for centuries. We happily watch and admire martial arts masters or yogi masters who have disciplined their minds and bodies, but we can also learn to use these capabilities in our everyday lives. From ancient times, methods of consciousness training have employed some sort of visualization techniques based on known data, creating mental laboratories in which students can safely discover and use new tools. The techniques create a virtual interface, like playing a computer simulation game.

By now, most people have heard about activities like "remote viewing," "psychic" or other abilities that rely on access to reality data using the larger field of consciousness. Although some people are gifted with the use of these abilities from a young age, everyone can learn the skills.

Our mind acts as a virtual interface to explore consciousness, make new discoveries, and change our real-life world.

Guided meditations, familiar to many people, use a variation of this to create a short-term virtual environment where participants can have access to previously invisible data and "out of the box" epiphanies, creations, and resolutions. Students are usually taught to construct a personal virtual interface structure, which they can visit regularly in meditation to develop strength and capabilities, resolve problems, and create outcomes to be manifested in the outer world.

Ancient mystery school curricula included this type of training, available only to higher level initiates because of its potential power. The name for the mental structure depends on the school or type of training. In older literature, the structure is often called the Palace of the Mind, Palace of Possibilities, or the Castle of Manifestation, among other names. A method I currently use calls this virtual interface a "workshop," which for me is a very comfortable way to understand and use it.[19] Within the virtual workshop structure, one is free to create and discover anything. I highly recommend training in this type of technique.

EMERGENCY RESOURCE TEST

After some years of study, discovery, and practice using my invisible resources, I found that I could actually use them in real-life situations. These phenomena did not just apply to famous New Age celebrities, nor were they parlor tricks. These were important skills and abilities in everyday life. I owned this power.

A real-life emergency offered me a dramatic test and confirmation of my resources. I came home one day in the fall and decided to close one of the large windows in my living area, as it was late afternoon and getting cold. My home was a loft with huge windows, about ten feet high and four feet across, and the window mechanisms were getting old. Thus, the windows were heavy and hard to open and close. The window faced east, overlooking the parking lot for my building. As I began to close it, it stuck a bit, so I gave a hard push, and down it came, but one finger was in the way and became painfully wedged between the window and the sill. Although the finger was not crushed, it was trapped. With only one hand free, I could not lift the huge pane. I began to panic.

The phone was too far away to reach. The apartment was quite soundproof, and the door, thirty feet away, was locked. What should I do? I knew that my neighbors would soon be coming home and parking in the lot, but would they see or hear me as I pounded on the thick window and yelled for help? *Wait a minute,* I told myself. *You know stuff. You can calm down and get out of this. You just have to shrink that finger and it will come out!*

I knew that Houdini was one person who had done lots of this, so although I had not been trained in any specific technique, I asked for help from my super-mind and called in Harry Houdini. I let him know I had no time for a lesson but had to shrink this finger pronto and pull it out. I knew I had to merge somehow with Houdini—or at least with the consciousness of his abilities. I was afraid but desperately determined. Suddenly, and without thinking, I felt myself take a deep breath and let it out, and I heard a voice in my mind say, *"That's right! Let all the breath out of that finger; deflate it."* The voice coached me for what seemed like minutes, but it was no doubt only a second or two. So I kept breathing out and relaxing that finger, and out it came with almost no effort! I almost passed out from relief.

This was an impressive demonstration of my body/mind interface in action. To me, the most remarkable feature was that my body instantly took the appropriate action before I was intellectually aware of any instruction. My innate wisdom knew what to do to save me. I just had to ask for it and stay open to allow my body/mind to implement.

I thanked Houdini, my body, my higher self, God, and everyone, and then realized that maybe I was injured! To my surprise, I was not injured at all—there was a small red mark on the affected finger that faded within hours. I knew this should have been an injury, perhaps a severe one. I was on my way!

AL'S STORY: CONNECTION CONFIRMATION

One dramatic experience stands out from my years of practice as confirmation to me that we possess almost miraculous abilities to connect with each other. This was my experience with a man named Al during his terminal illness and just after his death.

Al, the father of a friend, had terminal final-stage cancer, and was residing at home. Although I had never met or even seen a picture of Al, I knew he had been a great athlete and a real powerhouse. His decline was very sad and painful. I asked my friend if he could get permission for me to remotely visit Al to see if I could help. The next day, he said his mom and dad had agreed, and I started a regular morning remote visit to Al.

Early every morning, I would sit in meditation at the ocean's edge and ask to be connected with him. I would work mentally, projecting a sort of hologram of my vision of Al, even using my hands to clear away energy blockages or send him Reiki. His lungs were beginning to fail, and I remember one day going into the ocean and telling him that he would be okay, because in the water he did not need lungs to breathe. I let him know that he was underwater with me, and it seemed to calm him. Every day I got closer to him, and his energy "signature" was that of an old friend to me after several months. My connection speed became quite fast; I did not seem to need the words or connection protocols I had used at the beginning.

One early morning, I connected with Al as usual and began clearing energy when, suddenly, I was looking at a most impressive scene from inside my closed eyes. I was seated in a spacious room at a beautiful long maple wood table. I was looking out of a huge, two-story A-frame window onto a gorgeous dense forest just showing the first bright bits of fall color in the morning sunlight.

Where was I? I looked down and saw that I was seated on a wooden chair on a floral print pillow of some kind. When I looked at my legs, I was shocked, for my legs were withered and old in a pair of khaki shorts. Then I realized it—I was inside Al, looking out of HIS eyes! I was so startled I popped right out of the connection and back to my real world view of the sun and the ocean. I was quite shaken.

After I calmed down, I went back into my meditative state and thanked Al for allowing this intimate view. I went home and asked my friend to come over so I could ask some questions. I had never been to Al's home and knew nothing about it, so I did not tell my friend what had happened. I just asked questions. Does Al's house have a long maple table? Yes. Is there a huge A-frame picture window? Yes. Does it overlook a forest? Yes. As I asked each question, his face displayed more amazement. He kept asking, "How do you know this?"

My final question was about the pillow I saw underneath Al. "He has to sit on it, because he has almost no more flesh on his bottom," my friend said with tears in his eyes. He knew for sure that I was connecting. It was only a few more months before Al passed on, but I do believe our sessions gave him peace for his transition and some relief from pain.

Another significant confirmation of my connection with Al came on the day of his funeral. My friend told me the time and date of Al's funeral as he left to attend. On that day, I was not home but visiting my parents in New York, so I went to a favorite outdoor meditation spot to remotely attend Al's funeral. I was actually going to see if I could somehow show up at the ceremony, project a sort of hologram of myself there. I had joked with my friend that if he saw me, or some image of me, he should not be surprised.

The service was scheduled for 10:00 a.m., so I prepared myself a bit early, got into my meditative zone, and asked to be connected to the service. Instead, I was suddenly overwhelmed by the brightest light I have ever seen. This light seemed to be in me, around me, and encompassing everything in my consciousness. And while I basked in it, I heard Al say, "Thank you, Clare. I am not going to that funeral, and you don't need to go either. I am free, and I send you so much love." Tears just poured out of me while the light slowly withdrew. I thanked Al and God. Then, recovering myself, I got up and went home. That day, I experienced God through Al, and there is no greater gift. That day, I also learned that I could trust my capabilities, and that we truly are all one in the huge web of creation.

I hope that my experiences and discussion help readers to be more confident about exploring important consciousness frontiers. As we move into our renaissance, we need to develop clear guidelines to help students more easily access and use their own unique interfaces. This is an educational issue, a matter of providing information, support, and opportunity for practice.

I share a poem written by a friend in late 1990s after she was diagnosed with multiple sclerosis (MS). The medications currently used for MS were not available then, so she took none, and she still does not. Her poem speaks of her trust and commitment to listen and learn from her body/mind. By the way, although she is now a BodyTalk practitioner, she had not even heard of the system when she wrote and titled this poem.[20]

BODY TALK

my body shares the secrets
as i awaken inner gifts
always present, rarely seen
coming forward as awareness shifts
find the cause down deep within
still rooted firmly to effect
to find it search the quiet space
while pausing to reflect
realization floods the senses
and the truth will then be felt
the reality of the reasons
in the hand of life we're dealt
the language of the lessons
unfolding from within
will tell us all we need to know
when the healing will begin
where the answers can be found
what the process might entail
as we shed the layers of dis-ease
it's the truth that we unveil

© Jenna Schulman, 1999

8

External World: Life as a Learning Tool

Every person,
all the events of your life
are there because you have drawn them there.

What you choose to do with them
is up to you.

Richard Bach, *Messiah's Handbook*

Richard Bach reminds us that we create our external reality, and so we must decide how to make use of it. Although we can understand the external world as a construct on its own, it is also a reflection of us. What we create in the external world reflects clear messages back to us about facets of our own nature and power: all creation mirrors its creator. We can use the external mirror of our everyday life as an important device for seeing aspects of ourselves that may be otherwise invisible.

Our everyday world provides us with three-dimensional and sensual data that reflect our own nature, intention, desires, needs, and much more. Our everyday interface goes beyond the experience of a video screen or monitor, because we access our daily life in three-dimensional reality and with all our senses. Because we are so involved with the flurry of activity and re-activity in daily life, we need to learn to step back to recognize what might be crucial messages or teachings. Re-viewing the context of our everyday life from a different perspective helps us to take time out and discover the significance of events, relationships, or anything we may have called into our lives.

EVERYDAY LIFE AS INSTRUCTIONAL VIDEO

To achieve a more objective perspective that allows me to see the world of my daily life in new ways, I have adopted a conceptual frame: life as an instructional video, like watching YouTube in real life. This life-as-video perspective can be one of our most valuable renaissance tools.

To use the tool, just remind yourself consistently that *your life* reflects *you*. Your life is like a movie or some sort of interactive video game with periodic pop-ups that shows you the lessons or the key points about yourself. However, to discover these lessons, you have to be able to remove (literally re-move) yourself from participating in the drama going on around you. By doing this, you can better see its significance for you. Mind you, this exercise is not simply a left-brain analysis; it is very much a whole brain/body exercise.

To re-move oneself from the situational contexts of everyday life can be challenging. Especially in our culture, which values and emphasizes the minutiae of people's emotional lives, it is very easy to get caught up in the vortex of our own reactions. If we can just get over ourselves, literally, and try to see our situation objectively—like the YouTube video—we can learn a lot. Learning to switch into a more impersonal or aerial view also results in a confidence or calm that is a hallmark of command.

The mathematical phrase below is one I often use to help clients (and myself) understand or remember why things in our world might not be working as we like. If you are running into a stubborn issue in your work or life, use my handy behavioral equation to change things fast:

$D^2=G^2$

If you always do what you always did,
you always get what you always got.

We can use our external world events and cues (what we always got) to show us our own behavioral cause (what we always do).

Knowing this information allows us to reverse engineer and be able to discover what it is we are creating in the external world. The basic method works like this: Re-view your challenge issue (G) then determine what you are doing (D) when it happens. Shift any one behavior in D and the nature of G must change!

The external world provides an excellent resource through which we can receive information about ourselves that is normally invisible to us. All we have to do is shift the way we perceive or process that information, and take steps to alter unwanted outcomes. We can use our power to change much of our experience of the external world.

Your external world is a mirror for YOU. The person who most annoys you may reflect your most important lesson.

This creates a very important perspective shift. If everyone practiced this **re-vision** even once a day, can you imagine the difference? Some call this principle "mirroring," because people we call into our lives as clients, friends, partners, or neighbors mirror for us certain aspects of ourselves.

People mirror aspects or issues that were previously invisible to us, because, as we all know, it is hardest to see or hear ourselves. When we call someone in to provide us with this valuable mirroring service, however, they most often perform the service by irritating or angering us. This discomfort is also called "triggering."

One way I detect my most significant mirrors/lessons is by making a list of those people who are really triggering me right now—making me nervous, uncomfortable, angry, or annoyed. Once again, my emotional interface will send me messages. All I need to do is check in and detect how any element of my real-world "video" makes me feel. The stronger the emotion, the bigger the message.

Exercise:

The following steps provide a method you can use to practice shifting the D^2 G^2 equation for yourself.

Step One: Detection. The first step is to **replay any annoying or troublesome experience** in your mind or record your impressions after experiencing a problem.

1. **Ask some of the following questions:**
   - Does this type of thing keep happening around me repeatedly? (G^2)
   - What is similar about each time this happens?
   - How might this be reflecting something about ME? For example, if people are always angry with me, what am I angry about? If people are not listening to me, am I not listening to them?
   - How else might this problem be a mirror for me?
2. **Record your answers.** This exercise can be uncomfortable. We are all programmed to blame our life events on someone else. Make a list of behaviors you'd like to change.

Step Two: Change Just One Thing. This approach is focused and easy to remember. Changing one behavior forces all the other behavior around you to shift, so it can work wonders. Any habitual interpersonal pattern becomes like a dance we do by rote, our unconscious habitual moves cue the same dance pattern over and over. However, changing just one step in the dance forces the entire patter and rhythm to shift. Here's how to begin changing just one thing:

1. Based on your detection list, **choose one thing to change** for the next few days. For example, if people are not listening to you, maybe *you* are not listening.
2. **Brainstorm a list of ways you could change** the one behavior, in this case listening. To change listening behavior, you can ask more questions and listen more intently. To indicate you are doing this, say things like, "I hear you," or "I am listening." You can also reflect the other's words back to them saying, "That's really important. What I hear you saying is..." You may want to consult a resource on active listening techniques to get some other ideas.
3. Go out the next day with a priority i**ntention to make changes to that ONE behavior.** For listening, take every opportunity to use a new technique for active listening. Be extra observant of how others are behaving in response to this, and if others seem to be listening to you better even when you are not conscious of altering your own behavior.
4. **Record and reflect on your results.** Decide if you will

make further adjustments to your behavior, based on your results. If results are positive, you may decide to stay with the new behaviors that are working, and not add new variations. If you are not getting results, try at least one new behavior and see what happens.

5. **Repeat the exercise for one to two more days**, with any modifications or improvements, until you begin to notice changes. If you are NOT seeing changes, see if you can determine what it is about YOU that might still be in the way.
6. Try a **few more days with less focused effort.** Just state your positive intention at the beginning of your day. For example, "Today, I use active listening techniques, and people hear and listen to me." You have reprogrammed your behaviors so you will be doing your new techniques more or less automatically. In a week, see if you are "getting" something different than before. If so – you are ready to tackle another issue!

My experience is that by changing just one thing even for just one day, I can observe a lot of change. The external world acts as my screenplay, so I can go back home at night and write new language or actions into the script. If the movie still has the problem scenes, then I get to observe those scenes more closely and make further adjustments.

Manifestation Lessons

We know that manifestation surely ranks as one of the most popular topics in New Age literature, products, and services. Late twentieth century authors, teachers, and students did not invent this idea, but they certainly had a huge new market. I was one avid student of these techniques. Like many others, I studied from as many teachers as possible and put manifestation techniques into practice with great zeal. I learned some valuable lessons, mostly from the times when things did not work out quite as I had intended. I discovered that manifestation could be tricky, as I experienced several very important manifestation lessons. I share two of these in the sections that follow.

Premature Manifestation

During a peak period of study, I learned that if one was not fully ready to manifest something, then it would not fully or adequately appear. This is a universal law that only experience has taught me. I call it *premature manifestation.* If the person is not fully ready, the manifestation shows up briefly—like a preview. Like other premature events (smile), such a preview can feel disappointing.

Premature manifestation acts as a pre-view of our intentions, signaling that we are on the right track, but not quite ready for the full result.

One key example of this phenomenon for me was the premature manifestation of my first condo. I had initial success practicing manifestation techniques by creating positive affirmations using visualization and images of my creations to form a *treasure map.*[21] I carefully crafted language to affirm exactly what I intended. Then I created a collage on a large piece of poster board, with pictures depicting my intended creations, my picture in the center, and affirmations written in strategic places.

My first treasure map in Chicago had the following key components: a cool loft condo, with big windows and a city view; a tropical landscape where I envisioned a second home—the landscape picture had an ocean view with side pictures of palm trees and sky; my business card near the tropical scene, so it could move there, too; and pictures of people representing new clients. I also added features about my physical body that I wanted to re-form—I just cut out pictures of body parts I liked and put my head on them. I kept this map out in my living room, so I could look at it many times during the day, and affirm that it was already present in the now.

Since my loft condo was already on my map, I obviously figured it should manifest. However, my old beliefs about my worth or worthiness popped up to get in my way. I had just begun my business and had no real financial assets and some debt. It did not seem to me that I would be a good candidate for buying anything, but housing values were just starting to climb in the early '90s, and it was certain that anything one bought then would appreciate dramatically.

I was active in my community, so I knew lots of people. Through this network, I met the developer of my dream building. I completed a purchase application for a unit, developer-financed, and was within days on my way to owning my first condo. It happened so fast that

I actually turned it down. To this day, it boggles my mind, but it was just too soon. The condo could not yet manifest, because I had not yet fully embraced the aspects of my positive future as a present reality. My self-image was still constructed around beliefs that blocked my ability to manifest my dream home, even though I was using all the correct techniques.

My experience reinforced for me the need for better education in using our capabilities. If someone was coaching me, they might have been able to steer me through that dissonance sooner. I knew from my study that I must build from within first; then I would be ready to manifest in the outside world. My experience showed me that I had not done my internal building fully. So I got to work on myself inside, clearing and digging at whatever might be lurking to block me. As I studied, cleared, and trusted, I had more success manifesting.

The lesson of the condo pre-view was also a lesson about what has come to be called "poverty consciousness," a fear-based program about money that many of us have. In my generation, the program was installed and reinforced by parents and grandparents who almost daily recalled the horrors of the Great Depression and World War Two. I discovered that I was really chipping away at a very large belief system that had been manipulating my family and others for decades.

To work through this, I set about writing affirmations about how much money I had. I remembered the rules: write in the present tense; use all my senses to experience being rich; put all aspects of my vision on my map; and affirm the entire vision daily or even many times daily, and *feel* myself in the new reality as vividly as possible. This worked—to an extent. After all, I had been writing and speaking those affirmations, yet that first condo opportunity scared the daylights out of me. Obviously, the process of manifestation involved some pretty deep personal work, and I had learning to do.

I realized that I had to dig deeply to reveal my existing negative beliefs and accept that they existed. From there, I could change them. I could not simply assert a new positive belief without properly resolving conflicting beliefs that would sabotage manifestation. Learning techniques, such as Emotional Freedom Technique (EFT), helped me to make better progress with these shifts.[22]

This was a time of learning about shifts and balancing. In addition to learning more about shifting my inner world, I also learned how to navigate more smoothly between the world of alternative practices and traditional work environments. This involved learning to shift gears within myself, as I encountered different situations and had various types of experiences during the course of any day. It was exciting to be able to be present and see from several perspectives simultaneously. My corporate clients and many of my colleagues perceived a much different reality than I did, but I shared their reality too, especially when I was working with them.

I balanced these diverse realities by remembering they were different existential "zip codes." I reminded myself that during any day, I might visit places in several zip codes but return home to my own. Just because I visited the others did not force me to reside in them, nor did it mean that I gave up my home zone. Further, zip codes were value-neutral; they could all coexist without any being wrong. I was learning to live multi-dimensionally. Like any explorer, I was developing methods for navigating between and among interpersonal and self-worlds.

Interestingly, many clients seemed to know instinctively (Bob's Law) that I had additional information to share, and would ask me questions that were outside the scope of our work. One day a participant in a business communication workshop came to me at the break and asked if I could recommend a meditation class or resource. I had not mentioned anything about meditation to anyone in the group. Another asked me about Reiki for her shoulder. Again, the request just came out of the blue.

To keep myself steady and balanced during my early experiences of these simultaneous diverse worlds, I used journaling, meditating, and a time-out mechanism. During the day I would try to step out of the flow of events so I could assess and check my course. If I were at a client's, I might just take a short walk outside at a break, or go to an empty room, or even the ladies' room to reflect and re-focus. I also wanted to take a little time to appreciate and enjoy the many synchronicities and magic encounters I was having.

Meditation helped a lot, because it put me in touch with aspects of myself that were much more far-reaching, deeply knowing, and more capable than my ego-brain could ever be. I also learned that even if something did not show up instantly in my life, it would show up if I just kept focusing on it and asking if there were new tools I should be using, or beliefs I needed to clear. My experience taught me that our beliefs truly dictate how we manifest or achieve outcomes, and what those outcomes look like when they appear.

We may become discouraged about manifestation because we are trained to believe in only two extremes of the process: instant and easy or long and difficult.

Our belief system includes a sort of no-win clause about our own ability to manifest. We seem to believe that manifestation can only happen in one of two opposite ways: one is the easy, instant "lucky break," and the other is long hard work. Neither of these beliefs shows much trust in our power. We usually experience instant manifestation as external to our own agency—we purchase something or something is done to us or for us. One example would be taking medicine to alleviate symptoms of an illness. The other option is that we might just get lucky, which has nothing to do with our having or using our innate power.

The other belief about manifestation—the hard, uncertain, "99 percent perspiration"— is difficult and of course there are no guarantees of success. If we are too confident of success, that can be a negative as well. Our belief system tells us that we have to hope, and, of course— we must labor and struggle for what we want in life. Struggle, of course, has lots of polarity and not so much power. What I began to see was that there was a process at work that was neither instant nor long, and more importantly, it did not need to be at all arduous, which puzzled me no end.

The manifestation process seemed to simply require that I remain focused on the goal, and more importantly, that I not panic, but stay open and alert to new things in my world. This was a totally new way of accomplishing a goal; it was a new spin on concepts like performance, success, excellence—all my values were in flux. This process was synchronicity based on alignment of my intentions and my whole being with the flow of life. I experienced it as very uncomfortable, even though it was providing just what I wanted.

Despite feeling like I was doing nothing, somehow I was doing fine. Although my clients began to dwindle, I also noticed that I still had money. I was well supported on a lot less work than I logically should have needed. This felt really weird, because my relationship to money had not yet shifted out of the old belief system that "you have to work hard for what you get." It did not help that most of my friends were frantically working away at being traditionally successful in corporate or academic professions, and it was tough not to compare myself with them.

I was having a personal development dilemma. Although the New Age teachers all told me to trust and to let go, the prevailing paradigm in my career seemed to be about the opposite: striving for goals, making action plans, outperforming others, and climbing the mountain to success. I began to see that my external world was showing me that I had to be able to live in different zip codes even within myself. My internal landscape had old and new worlds and lots of scary frontiers. I had to take time to sort this out, and take it easy on myself.

When I was ready, I finally manifested the loft condo that I pictured. Interestingly, the picture on my map more closely resembled the preview condo, but features of it did manifest in the real loft. What happened next proved yet another important phenomenon—manifestation time lag—or what I also call "wobbling."

MANIFESTATION WOBBLING

My experiments with the study and practice of manifestation taught me how frustrating it can be to live in the old world while you are in process to manifest a new one. I found out that during this awkward process, things seemed to wobble along, moving in slow motion or backward or not at all. Then suddenly, they just happened—fast. Movement was incremental for ages, then poof! Everything shifted exponentially.

Knowing about this incremental time lag, and that it is not permanent, is especially important for people now, as most of us are undergoing significant transitions fraught with discomfort. If we have done what we can to clarify our intentions and align our actions, manifestation does happen. And when it does, it is often in an unexpected exponential way. My first experience of this happened during my last year in Chicago, as I continued to meditate, focusing on my new world as present in the now – the tropical setting, the ocean, the new clients, and all the great items on my treasure map.

I finally manifested my loft condo and things were going well. However as I affirmed my new tropical world daily, many aspects of my "real" world in Chicago began to disappear. No one told me this was going to happen! It was very uncomfortable; I had to calm myself and try to grasp what was happening. While I had met a few teachers, and made contact with my higher consciousness, I was still on my own amid shifting worlds. Those of you who have had this experience know how scary and lonely it can be.

To keep hearing from so many New Age teachers that "things happen just as they should," or that "there are no accidents," annoyed me a lot during these times when life seemed to offer me only two disappointing choices: a vanishing world on the one hand and a world that had not yet manifested on the other. I tried hard to feel peaceful and enlightened when I was actually just afraid and crabby.

Manifestation "wobbling" occurs in transitional phases when your old reality has left, but the new things have not come in yet. This period can be challenging.

I want to explain exactly how this transitional phase worked for me, as it may help people who either are or will soon be in this process. The shift out of my old world required that the three-dimensional, physical trappings of my external world interface—like clients, friends, income, even my office—had to leave to make room for the new reality I had created. Who knew? This was all part of an incremental transition that would soon result in an event causing an exponential shift.

My transition began when clients I had been working with for years began to feel they no longer needed my services. I was not replaced by some competitor; they just had no more need. At the height of my small business, I probably had ten regular clients. Over a period of a year, I went down to one, and that was sporadic. Nothing I did would turn up new business in Chicago either, and, of course, my heart wasn't in it because I was already in the new world, although not consciously. How would I survive?

I continued to meditate daily, affirm my intentions, and let go as best as I could. I continued to do my energy exercises, to keep my discipline, to stay open and trust, but I was bewildered. In addition to my clients leaving, my friends began floating away. Same idea—no quarrels or issues, they simply began to move in different circles or moved physically away, until I was down to two out of eight or ten pretty close friends. I did realize as well that I was no longer a fit with most of my old friends. They annoyed me, and their frequencies seemed to irritate my whole being or make me unbearably sad. Even though I could read things that explained this process, it was extremely disturbing. I was not having fun.

The last straw was when I lost my lovely office downtown, which was at least allowing me to believe that I was still a professional person with standing. Same way—no bad feelings, no financial issues, but the organization from which I was sub-leasing needed the office space for their own expansion. I was given a week to leave. Things were moving faster.

I had to pack up all my books, files, office equipment, and furniture, and move everything out and into my loft in a week. And I did it. It was crowded but I made it fit. Exhausted and confused, I sat there and asked, "Why?" No answer. There was my new world treasure map broadcasting my not-yet manifested future. There was all the stuff from my current de-constructing world. And there I sat in a heap on the floor.

Weeks passed. Somehow, I kept my routine; it was all I had. I exercised like a maniac, I meditated, I journaled, I read, I cried. Then one day, out of the blue, my phone rang. It was a friend and colleague who lived in Miami and owned a business that had added many new staff members to meet rising client demand. Because of the larger, more diverse employee group, the organization was experiencing growing pains and needed some assistance. Could I come down? I tried to sound calm and professional. Of course I would!

This was truly a co-incidence. Parts of my life were coming together to create a new picture, mirroring the one on my map. After all, I had placed my business card in the tropics, with some pictures of new people. I had not seen my friend in a year or so, but we had been involved for almost a decade in an alumni advisory group that met for three days at least twice a year, so we had often shared ideas and information about our lives and work. That one telephone call began a series of events that allowed me to "discover" and come to love Miami, and I moved my whole life there. Not much more than a year later, I would be living in South Beach—and have a view much like the one on my map.

What I learned ultimately was that trust and letting go or surrender (in the good sense) are built over time. One sees incremental manifestation before one sees the whole enchilada as it were. The trick is to make it through the incremental part without giving up, or the enchilada will never appear. I coined a phrase for this transitional manifestation process: "It's incremental until it goes exponential!" I say this to myself and my clients to this day when the incremental part seems to be taking forever. Remember: do not give up if things seem to be taking more time to change than you would like, even though (like I was) you are doing your part. You are preparing the stage for a shift that can happen instantly at any time!

It's incremental . . . until it goes exponential!

My move to Miami Beach demonstrated beyond a doubt that "it's incremental till it goes exponential." When it does—look out! I have never fallen in love with a place before, so I didn't really know what was happening to me. Additionally, despite all the wild crazy things one hears about South Beach, what stole my heart was quite different. It was truly the energy and life of the place—the actual interface. I knew it felt a bit extreme to cry every time I left, and I knew that I had never longed for a place like that, but I came to realize that I was meant to be there. All my message systems told me so.

My work kept me returning to Miami and staying on the beach. As I deepened my relationship with the beach, my ties to Chicago fell away faster, and the universe somehow conspired to make everything happen extremely easily.

Synchronicities flowed faster and more frequently, proving to me that outward systems were all working optimally to reflect my own inner movement. I obtained a part-time position in Miami so I had enough income to get my practice up and running. My Chicago condo sold fast and, with only a small advertisement in my condo lobby, my neighbors flocked to purchase all the furniture I wanted to sell. Before I knew it, I was driving south in a loaded car, leaving my home of twenty years for the wilds of a new world I had never even considered just a few years before.

Synchronicity: Observing the Dots Connecting

I believe that synchronicity is the experience and outward manifestation of integrated whole-being alignment. Synchronicity demonstrates the 99% invisible rule: it shows us that our intentions, thoughts, and actions have aligned to create an easy flow of optimal outcomes.

Synchronous outcomes are often called co-incidences, opportunities, or even accidents (which can be positive as well as negative). One popular New Age maxim is that "there are NO accidents; everything happens for a reason." This thought can be especially annoying when bad or hurtful things happen to us, but I believe that there is always a reason or a lesson, no matter how bad things seem. It's easy for all of us to deny any part in a negative situation but gleefully take credit for a positive co-incidence or opportunity!

Synchronicity is real co-incidence. Events flow effortlessly and you simply "go with the flow."

The dots of life can connect themselves. My move to Miami Beach ushered in a flood of synchronicities to help me learn more about alternative health and healing modalities. Although I had discovered many resources and met teachers in Chicago, once in Miami Beach, I was offered direct access to experiences and teachers I had only previewed before my move.

My first huge experience of this level of synchronicity involved meeting Donna Eden and learning energy medicine. I had literally fallen onto the work of Donna Eden while I was still in Chicago. One day, at my favorite New Age bookstore, I was in the alternative health aisle and a book fell out right at my feet. I almost tripped on it. Picking it up, I saw it was the first edition of *Energy Medicine*,[23] which could not have been out for more than a few months.

I remember clearly looking at Donna's picture in the back of the book and hearing myself say, "I know you! I am going to meet you soon, sister!" I thought, *Well, I guess part of me knows something.* I took the book home and loved it so much that I almost memorized it. I did the energy medicine daily routine every day in Chicago, but I did not give any thought to how I would meet Donna. I felt like it had already happened.

After a few months in Miami Beach, I was looking for a new primary care physician and dentist when my opportunity to meet Donna Eden occurred. At my local health food store, I noticed a flyer for an alternative health fair the next Saturday at a nearby university campus. A holistic dentist was giving the keynote. I needed a dentist, so I decided to go.

When the day came for the event, I didn't want to go. It was a miserable day; rain poured down in sheets. Although I desperately wanted to stay home in bed, my inner voice was nagging me to go. So I dressed and pushed myself grudgingly out the door.

In other synchronous experiences, I was right on time for an event despite many delays, but for this one I was very late, or so it seemed. By the time I got to the university, found the building, parked far away, and trudged through the downpour, the dentist's presentation was over, and he was gone. So, I thought, this must be about something else. Soaking wet and cranky, I still knew I should stay to see why the heck I was there. I wandered up to a table and vaguely looked at a sign that I soon realized said, DONNA EDEN IS COMING TO MIAMI! SIGN UP HERE! I began laughing hysterically. Bingo! That was why I was here. I registered for the event immediately.

I attended my first Eden Energy Medicine workshop and many more. I got to know Donna and her husband David Feinstein, and I am grateful for all that I learned. Eden Energy Medicine also introduced me for the first time to a strong health matrix—a global community of healers and people committed to discovering new frontiers of human capability. Donna and David were the first teachers and leaders I met who were committed to building a global matrix. In fact, if you look on their Innersource website today, the tag line reads, "Raising the Vibration of the Planet, One Person at a Time."[24]

As if just meeting Donna was not enough, my synchronicity extended further. One day, after I had been studying energy medicine for about a year, I walked into our condo office with Donna's book, *Energy Medicine*, in my hand. In the office, I encountered an older Latin man whom I had never thought to be a student of alternative healthcare or anything like it. When he looked at the book, his eyes grew wide, and he began pointing and exclaiming, "It's the boook! The boook! You have the boook!" He grabbed my hand, insisting we go to his apartment so he could show me he had "the book," too. He related he had a friend who had studied with Donna (he proudly showed me Donna's autograph on the inside). What was the chance of this?

A few months later, I was able to introduce this man to Donna in person, which was also an event that defied all odds. Just the meeting of those two, and the fact that I could facilitate it, proved to me that we are all connected in this synchronous world. Once we set things into motion in a certain direction, we can expect the unexpected.

Another synchronous stream of events in Florida facilitated my study of Reiki.

For many years, I had received hints that I would eventually study and practice Reiki. At least three people I met in holistic health classes assumed I was a Reiki master. Each time, I would say, "No, I am not," and, each time, the person would laugh and say something like, "Well, not yet, maybe." A young massage therapist in New York put her hands on me and immediately chirped, "You are a Reiki master!"

Experiences like this always made me think of my sci-fi hero, Doctor Who, and his escapades moving through the time/space continuum. In one adventure, Doctor Who sets his time machine for certain coordinates, but, as usual, ends up in a completely different time and place—this time in the prison of a slave spaceship. Striking up a casual conversation with one of the prisoners, he tells the young man how much he likes the man's beautiful home planet and city. "Oh, you've been there?" asks the prisoner. Doctor Who replies cheerily, "Oh, yes, but not yet." "Yes but not yet" has become like a mantra for me when I begin receiving clues or messages that give a pre-view of future events.

With all these messages about my future coming to me from others in the world, I trusted that Reiki was a "not yet" and would show up. And it did. Once I was settled in Miami Beach, I began thinking more about Reiki and decided I would get a book on it. Just as Donna's book found me in Chicago, Diane Stein's *Essential Reiki* found me in a Miami bookstore. The book fell off the shelf and hit me on the shoulder.[25]

Stein had taken a big leap in publishing this book, because the Reiki symbols had been kept as a major mystery school-type secret for most of the twentieth century. Nevertheless, she provided the symbols, with explanations and step-by-step instructions for drawing them. I still did not know many folks in Miami, so I wasn't sure how I would meet the right Reiki master to receive my training and attunement. Thanks to synchronicity, it took only about a week.

I was asked to attend a business networking luncheon. I do not normally like such events, but after 9/11, I needed clients. I arrived at the luncheon and looked for a seat. I chose one seat, then changed my mind and moved to the next table, in a seat right behind my original choice. A woman came in and took my original seat. I greeted her, and we introduced ourselves. "What do you do?" I asked. "Well, mostly I am a Reiki instructor," she replied. Her next level one Reiki class was two days away, so I signed up and off I went. Although I had not known it beforehand, that was the networking I went there to do!

The synchronicity continued. During this time of intense learning about alternative health, I had another pre-view of my future—an initial introduction to the BodyTalk System, which I was "not yet" ready to study at that time.

Here's how the pre-view happened. As I was learning Eden Energy Medicine, I incorporated the energy medicine routine into my daily morning meditation and yoga on the beach. Most days, I saw the same folks out at that time, including my neighbor Susan. She asked what I was doing, and I told her I was studying with Donna. She said, "You should try BodyTalk! It's wonderful." She was becoming certified as practitioner and described the system.[26]

Susan gave me a session so I could experience BodyTalk, and I was very impressed. When she asked if I had any issue I wanted to address, I showed her some red dots that had been popping up on my skin. The BodyTalk practitioner ascertains priorities from the client's body/mind by using applied kinesiology to obtain yes/no answers as she works through a detailed protocol. In my case, body chemistry came up, and Susan asked me, "Do you wear a scent?" I said no, then she asked, "Do you use a laundry detergent that has a scent?" I said yes, and she indicated I might want to stop using it. I did so and in two days the dots were gone.

Of course, I went on the web and looked up BodyTalk. When I saw the picture of BodyTalk founder John Veltheim, I had very much the same reaction as when I had first seen Donna Eden's picture—"I know you!" This early introduction to BodyTalk was another good example of a pre-view—I was ready to be aware of the system, but not yet ready to participate. Nevertheless, BodyTalk kept intersecting my life. I would keep meeting people who knew about it or had had a session. I did not have time to study yet another modality, so I put BodyTalk on the back burner. Several years later, I began actively studying and became certified to practice.

Before concluding the discussion of synchronicity, I want to describe some of the signals I get from my internal guidance system to tell me that synchronicity is occurring. This may help someone who is learning their own body/mind signals, because as we have seen, messages often arrive in unfamiliar formats.

We have all experienced a time when we set out to do one thing, then sort of forgot about that goal and ended up doing something else. This is not old age setting in. What seems to be happening is that the conscious chattering mind has sort of switched off for a bit, and another part of the interface guidance system has control. The trick seems to be just to go with it. I believe that when I lose my manic goal orientation and let myself be smoothly guided, much better outcomes occur, and those otherwise impossible things just show up.

Most important discoveries have come when something happened that was unplanned. Books and pamphlets just fell on me. I went to the wrong places or arrived late for intended events and just happened into people. Most of the time, optimal outcomes are the results of my doing something other than I intended, waiting until what should have been too late, or having to go back to the house because I forgot something. When such things happen, I have learned to be very optimistic. Something really good is about to occur.

Synchronicity delivers outcomes without what we think of as work or achievement.

We are trained to plan and implement, to diligently focus on achieving sequential goals and outcomes through personal agency. How surprising to find that planning in the traditional sense cannot create or force synchronous results. Instead, intention and trust combine to form a much less polarized form of agency that seems to allow all probabilities to partner with us.

To create the conditions for synchronicity, I have learned to let go and ask my higher self or super-mind to take control. The results can be astonishing. When both my parents were in their final years, my visits to them were stressful. On one visit, I needed a break badly, so I got into my rental car, took a deep breath, and said, "Dear higher self, this car is my vehicle, and I am our vehicle. I'll drive the car, you drive me, please. Take us to the best spot now for some rest and healing."

I headed out with no real destination in mind, and found myself driving a familiar road to a small village downtown area. I had been there many times to shop or get a coffee, but this time, I didn't even notice the usual landmarks. Instead, I spotted a jewelry store. Although the store had been there for many years, right across the street from my favorite coffee shop, I had never noticed it. I parked across the street, looked at the store display window, and saw a man behind the window cheerily waving at me. I had never seen this man before.

He buzzed me in, and we introduced ourselves. We both felt like we had been friends for years. I said that I was interested in jewelry, but also in stones, and looked up on the store mezzanine to see a huge collection of raw stones, rocks, geodes—all giving off tons of energy. "Can I see those stones?" I asked. "Of course! That's my passion," he replied. We spent an hour or so together, and he gave me a healing stone, which I still have and cherish. We stayed in touch for years, and his friendship helped me through that very difficult time.[27] Experiences like this have given me confidence to use my innate guidance system and enjoy synchronicity.

9
Accessing the Power of Earth

Everything can talk to you if you listen. Everything is self-explanatory. Before it was explained, Nature was there.

Juliu Horvath

Nature speaks to us clearly and effortlessly throughout life, as Juliu Horvath points out.[28] Just as our bodies convey and send messages in many diverse formats, so the body on which we live—the earth—functions as an immense, diverse portal to power. We just have to tune in and listen.

Much is written and taught about knowing the ways of the earth. This knowledge has been retained and passed down to indigenous people from ancient cultures who had learned to access the power of the earth and the entire natural world. Like learning about the invisible resources of our own bodies, our renaissance regarding the power of Nature and Earth is a re-discovery of this wisdom, a new "seeing" of very old and sacred ways. As we begin to explore the natural world, our individual journeys often include crucial discoveries that echo ancient, mythological, and archetypal journeys of initiation and rebirth.[29]

Once we have experienced moments of expanded perception at any site on earth, we can never relate to the body of our Mother Earth in the same way. This type of knowing surpasses education; it becomes reverence. Such knowledge is a trust of a living power that seems beyond our everyday reality, but which is with us and available to us at all times.

For years, New Age students and practitioners have been called "tree huggers," not just because they tend to be environmentalists, but because they may actually hug trees to connect with them. I highly recommend this! Trees and all plants are alive, and they do communicate. Anyone can experience this by just being open to it. Most gardeners and plant owners will tell you that when they talk to their plants the plants thrive. Studies like Masaru Emoto's water research further prove that our intentional transmissions, in words, emotions, and even sound, affect all living things. Our earth receives all of our transmissions every day and demonstrates the effects—positive or negative.

Many people can actually see the earth's energy field and thus can access the lines of energy—sometimes called "ley lines." However, one can feel the energy of a place even without visual cues. Everyone has been to a beach and had to decide on that perfect spot to spend the day. Some spots just feel better than others, and you know when you get the right one. If you settle in the wrong one—maybe because you think you should go there or someone else likes it better—most likely you will be uncomfortable and may even move. This happens also in restaurants, homes, everywhere, because everything is alive with energy.

Messages from the Earth

Throughout my renaissance, I have received messages and experienced new realities just by being in certain places on the earth. These co-incidences always seemed timed perfectly to help me on my journey or lead me to other discoveries. Often, they occurred in places well-known as power spots, sacred places, or energy vortexes, but discoveries happened for me at many other places as well.

Any place on the earth can provide views of new worlds, if we are open to explore.

As I studied more about sacred or special places on the planet, I began to get urges to go on journeys of discovery to ancient or sacred sites. My own personal explorations demonstrated to me that the earth, and particular places on it, acted as interfaces to invisible frontiers. I traveled to known places with established history. I obtained detailed site maps and explanatory information, but what I discovered in these places was not on the maps. The places, the earth itself, acted as a portal for me to experience more levels of myself and of a previously unknown world.

Of course, I had read about the special energy vortex spots on our planet, but somehow I discovered the phenomenon in ways that seemed crafted just for me. I found that these spots interact with our own being so that we access power in whatever way is best for us. Also, I discovered that energy spots might be well-known, like Stonehenge, New Grange, Sedona, or the Great Pyramid, or they might be anywhere on the earth. The lesson for me was to remember to connect with the earth and to be alert to her message signals.

Although not in the same way as Columbus or Magellan, I surely found out that worlds existed beyond what I had been told. At one point in my study, I felt called to go to the American southwest and explore the ancient Native American civilization called the Anasazi. I went out there for years on every vacation, haunting ruins and climbing around red rocks, often in places I probably should not have been. I just followed my felt sense of what to do. I felt I was being called by the ancient people. It was during one of these trips that I had my first spontaneous experience of another life or dimension, and it came as I made contact with an earth artifact.

I was visiting Canyon de Chelly National Monument in Arizona and was at one of the visitors' spots overlooking the canyon. It was evening, and most tourists had already left the site, so I was pretty much alone. I was drawn to sit down on a particular rock overlooking the canyon because it looked like a chair to me, formed with perfect indentations for someone to sit. The moment I sat and made contact with the rock, I was catapulted into another reality.

I found myself sitting there (or somewhere), looking out from different eyes on a different scene. I looked down into a canyon below only to see hundreds of people all looking up at me. They were all ages, genders, and sizes in what looked like native clothing of indeterminate origin. They were dark-haired and dark-skinned. They were expecting something from me. I could feel their sadness and their neediness.

But who was I? I tried to get a clue from how I was dressed. Looking down, I saw that my chest was completely covered in a golden metal necklace or breastplate, which reflected the bright sun with an almost blinding glare. I had brown skin and strong arms, which were bare. There was also something heavy on my head that hung down the sides of my face, but I could not really see it. I could hardly move anyway because the whole thing was so frightening. The energy of the people was very intense—like an urgent pleading, although they were eerily silent.

Panicked, I asked out loud to no one special, "What do they want?" I heard a calm voice say, "They need your blessing, dear one." Although I had no idea how to bless all these people or what that would do for them, I did my best to say some words and send them huge love from my heart. I spread out my strong arms to encompass them and boom! I returned to sitting on the plain old rock, arms still outstretched. It took me a while to be able to get up and try to walk; I was shaken and felt dizzy. What had happened to me?

I began to realize that I had made a connection with these ancient people by contacting the land. Their energy was not gone; it was very present, and so much more than any tour guide or literature was telling me. A second occurrence on this same trip confirmed my growing awareness that the earth was actively sending me messages.

As you may know, in the American southwest you can drive many miles on the long desert roads through flatness that seems to go on forever. In this landscape, buttes and mesas appear as tiny silhouettes and slowly grow larger. Even though you are going 100 miles per hour, the things seem to stay in the far distance for hours until at one moment they are a real size. You see so much of this that it becomes like a backdrop. Even though it may seem to be simply scenic, I found that the landscape can send a pretty dramatic message.

As I drove north toward an ancient ruin site called Aztec in New Mexico, I saw dozens of such formations, but one particular configuration caught my eye, and I began to look at it intensely, it looked so familiar. Then I began to cry uncontrollably. I had no idea why I was crying, but my emotional body apparently did, and I could not stop the tears. I could not tell if they were tears of joy or sadness. But there I was, speeding down the long road, sobbing.

I knew that answers would come if I could remember to ask. I was still a bit self-conscious about this, as we are taught not to talk to ourselves, but then I figured—who cares? Here I was in the middle of nowhere by myself. So, I asked, "Why am I crying like this? What are these mesas to me?"

Then a voice inside me said, *"This is how you know you are almost home."* The phrase "*almost home, almost home*" kept repeating in my head as the tears poured out for miles. I began to realize that I had been here before and that I had traveled long distances away from here and returned with great emotion. But who was I? Where had I been? Where was home?

Answers to these questions took a while to come in. They arrived later that year through my dreams. One night, months after I had returned to my home in Chicago, I began to dream about a new activity for me: running. Night after night, I ran in my dreams, and I ran with a very specific purpose.

In the dreams, I was a muscular, brown-skinned man, and I ran many miles across terrain that included jungles, deserts, and mountains, and it was usually very hot. I carried some sort of package as I ran. The delivery of the package was important, although I never really saw the actual package or knew what it held. I also never saw the delivery, but I knew that I was doing this as a job.

As I began to ask questions in my morning meditations, the dots began to connect themselves back to my earlier New Mexico experience. The whole picture just bubbled up one day when I was meditating. Sort of like a UPS or FedEx delivery guy, I was a courier runner in an ancient civilization. The mesas that made me cry were my geographic signposts that I was "almost home." This would have been important because if you run, you know that you can enter a "zone" and let go of your real-world orientation. Especially in a very long distance run, being able to use earth's landscape cues to know your location would be extremely helpful. The mesas interacted with the runner's emotional body like a natural GPS signal.

Once I got the answers to explain my experience, two things happened: I got some new running shoes and started happily running for the first time in my life, and the dreams stopped. The message had been delivered. Once I realized that this message had such importance, I wanted to learn more, so I did some further research.

When I researched the possibility that ancient delivery runners like the one in my dream actually existed in the American southwest and in other parts of America, I got solid confirmation and leads to new places to explore. Before the horse was brought to our continent by Spanish explorers, native people traded with distant neighbors in North and Central America two ways: by boat—both on rivers and oceans—and by foot, running over land. The man I connected with was a runner, and he went from the desert southwest of the United States all the way into the jungles of what is now Mexico. I was fascinated to remember that I first got the messages about this on my way to a site ironically named Aztec, a name I thought was odd for a site with no relationship to Mexico.

Further research led me to fascinating documentation describing the artifacts from the Yucatan peninsula in Mexico that have been found not only in the American southwest, but as far north as Wisconsin. Researchers have followed clues to reveal many ancient American trade and migration routes.[30]

My experiences in Arizona and New Mexico were just two of the many discoveries that happened almost automatically once I began actively using my power resources. Not only was this fun, but with each experience I gained confidence that I possessed very sophisticated and ancient equipment. Using this innate power allowed me to discover more features of myself and opened doors for me into a world I never knew was there.

Researching any message you receive can produce exciting new discoveries.

It is very easy now to use the huge, instant resource of the Internet. There are two excellent reasons to do such research: first, it is confirmation that you can trust your abilities; second, your research may be the way to lead you to another discovery. That's certainly how it has worked for me.

Being open to earth data also helped me discover that many powerful earth portals exist besides the famous ones we read about and see on TV specials. One of these little-known places was near my parents' retirement community in New York State. The spot is now a park, with a popular running and bike path that curves for miles through beautiful forest and meadow land along a creek. I ran on this path every morning or evening when I visited my parents.

When I first started going to the park, I was drawn to a mound-like structure on the path. I would lie on the earth there and feel very close to the people who once inhabited the place, members of what we know as the Iroquois Nation. Those native people called the place a name that literally translates into English as "level heaven," but I think it meant "heaven on earth." The whole place always felt magical to me, and it seemed right that the local government had worked to preserve it as a natural place for recreation.

In this place, I received messages from almost every aspect of the land, especially from the trees, with whom I talked on every visit. For those of you who have not tried communicating with trees, I highly recommend it. The method is pretty simple. You just go up to one that catches your attention and touch it or—yes—you can hug it! You should feel something very quickly, and you may get messages in any of the ways we have reviewed. The trees in the park communicated to me through felt sense, and the messages were of comfort, support, and even healing. There was a feeling of great wisdom there and much history.

One day while visiting, I got confirmation that I was not the only one who knew about these talkative trees. While talking to one of my favorite trees I called "Grandfather," a man appeared, as if from nowhere. He was bearded and looked professorial, dressed not in athletic gear or running clothes but with khaki trousers and a clean but rumpled print shirt. He approached me and said, "I see you like the trees. They are very friendly here." I said I agreed, and he showed me his favorites, which included Grandfather, and three trees I called The Sisters.

He asked if I had experienced any messages or feelings up the path that cut through a more densely wooded area. I said, "Yes, I think there are fairies there. I can feel them, but they have not shown themselves to me." He lit up and smiled broadly. "Oh, yes, they are there. I have not spoken to them, but my wife does!" Acting much like the former TV detective called Columbo, he asked for my email, pulling a pencil stub and a scrap of paper out of his shirt pocket. After we said goodbye, I turned for a split second to look at Grandfather Tree. When I turned to watch my new friend walk away, he had just vanished!

There was no rational explanation. I saw him set out in a direction; there was no way he could have gotten out of my visual field in that or any other direction, walking or even running. He was just gone. I got the goose bumps and started laughing. Messages were coming in. By the way, he never emailed me.

Experience showed me the power of the earth and the seamless way a place could speak to me. If I paid attention to the messages from all of my interfaces and asked questions, I would be led to discoveries of new worlds wherever I was. My enhanced trust and awareness of the earth helped me greatly on my trip to my new world of South Florida. My expanded awareness worked like an innate GPS that directed me to the perfect places and experiences.

Earth Direction and Support

On the trip from Chicago to Miami Beach, I did not plan my stops. Instead, I asked to be led clearly to those places that would be most useful or helpful for me. I was guided perfectly by intentionally connecting my innate guidance system to that of the earth herself. Then I just relaxed and drove.

I arrived in Georgia, thinking I should stop somewhere, when the sign came up for Macon. I knew nothing about Macon, yet I automatically exited at the rest area marked TOURIST INFORMATION, as if someone else were driving my car. Once in the information building, I was greeted by a lovely Southern lady with white hair, a sweet little suit, and pearls. "Looking to stay the night in Macon?" she asked, and I automatically replied yes, even though I had no idea why. She enthusiastically showed me the brochures, pointing out one old mansion converted into a B&B that she especially liked. We called and they had a room.

Macon was spared by Sherman on his destructive Civil War "March to the Sea" and thus retains one of the loveliest collections of antebellum homes in the United States. But my journey of discovery in Macon took me to a much different and more ancient world of the early native people of that place. The white-haired lady spent only a little time on the mansion tours, then led me to a rack where my eyes lit up as I gazed on brochures depicting an ancient mound site called Ocmulgee, now part of the National Parks Service. I happily realized that this was why I was guided here.

I stayed in Macon for two days, and spent hours each day at the Ocmulgee site, which spoke to me of its human history and its healing power. The place relaxed me after all my hectic moving, financial activities, and travel. The earthworks and mounds spoke to me of stability; the earth spoke to me of support. As I lay on the soft green grass, it was like being held by the Mother Earth herself. I felt as if I was being assured that my journey would go well, and that I was safe, supported, and never alone.

Once more, the earth herself acted as my interface, not only to the wisdom of these ancient ones but to an entire suite of messages of support and love that I received at all levels—mental (I had thoughts, like words of support), emotional (I felt waves of emotion that resulted in tears but were not sadness), physical (my whole body tingled and I felt waves of what I can only call love, but it was like warmth without heat), and spiritual (the aggregate experience). As always, connecting with the earth helped me to "ground" and to confirm my path on all levels while providing me an incomparable feeling of support and pure love.

Learning to Access Earth Portals

Ways to access the knowledge and beauty of our earth are unlimited. To tap into the earth itself, or any specific place on the earth, requires making contact. I like to make as much physical contact as possible with the spot or feature I choose. Then I just let the messages come in. Here's how you can try it.

Exercise:

1. **Find a place in nature** that appeals to you or calls you. Make sure you have allowed enough time for yourself to really connect with this place.
2. **Contact the earth** with your body. Touch the earth or natural feature (tree, rock, water). Connect with it as much as possible.
3. **Visualize yourself becoming one with this feature** of the earth, and so with all of the earth. You may want to state an affirmation. I usually say, "I connect myself with my Mother Earth, my whole being to her whole being."

4. **Recognize and thank those who have been here before you**, and whose spirits may still reside here. They may have a message for you.
5. You can **ask for messages, or just be still and let the place speak**. Pay attention to all your "displays." You may have physical sensations or feel a wave of emotion. You may hear enhanced natural sounds or even hear words. There is no wrong way to experience this connection.
6. **You can ask for any message to be made clearer**, if you are not sure what you are getting. I learned that although I felt ridiculous when I first started to ASK, it worked! Remember, you are exploring.
7. **Do not worry or stop if you experience pushback within yourself**. We have all been trained that doing such a thing is ridiculous, and we are imagining the whole thing. The trick here is to let the pushback messages come and drift through.
8. **You can use an audio recorder to record your experience.** If you record the actual event, you could be surprised at what you hear when you replay it. I have heard some very curious sounds and also found I had forgotten things that I was experiencing. Do not do the recording if you think it will distract you or make you self-conscious. The point is to connect, not perform.
9. **You will know when your experience is complete.** Of course, you can also ask. Before leaving, I try to remember to thank the earth or place and all those who reside there.
10. **After the experience, write or record your results.** Also pay attention to your dreams and any messages that may surface when you meditate or journal. More information or clarification often comes later, as you process the event.

This basic process works anywhere, and you will alter it to suit your style and needs. You can use it with any natural feature, like a tree or rock, a stream, the ocean, or any earth feature. You can also use a variation of it for a sacred or special place and its artifacts. The point here is to explore and enjoy. You may be amazed at what new vistas you can access in a world you thought you already knew.

In addition to contacting the earth or a place, you can also get good information from artifacts of nature. Indigenous people have always revered natural artifacts, such as feathers, stones, and other natural objects. Such artifacts can really "talk" to us if we are open to it. There are many excellent resources on the powers of crystals and stones. One of my favorite books is entitled *Love is in the Earth.*[31] Collecting stones and crystals need not be expensive, but it is enjoyable, and can be very useful.

For example, my jeweler friend in Buffalo gave me a wand-shaped piece of a beautiful blue stone called kyanite. I loved it immediately but had no idea what to use it for. I read the entry in Melody's book, but it seemed to me that this stone had more to offer. One day, about a year after I received the stone, I developed a huge sore pimple on my chin. Suddenly, for no logical reason, I found myself reaching for the kyanite. I just began to hold it on the blemish. After about ten minutes of holding the stone in place, the redness and swelling was almost gone. The pimple went away totally after two more applications of the stone. Since then, I never travel without that stone.

If you are drawn to stones, you may also want to make sure you pick one up whenever you go to a special spot on the earth. These artifacts can help you to re-connect with a special place and your experiences there. Earth artifacts may also have other gifts—just ask. Staying open to nature's power portals can produce magical renaissance results.

Part Three
Challenges to Power

Introduction

If I could have convinced more slaves that they were slaves, I could have freed thousands more.

Harriet Tubman

The expansive world of invisible resources has a darker side. I would like to wade into that murkier water and explore some of the hidden agendas that act to weaken our power from outside or within us. Our individual and collective human power resources are conscripted daily and often sabotaged or manipulated at levels below our awareness. Unless we become aware of these powerful challenges, we cannot be free.

Because our emotional power resources comprise such a rich asset, we can look there first to discover vulnerabilities. Emotions, as we have seen, are often repressed, avoided, or controlled because of their primal force. The same force of passion that allows an artist or athlete to achieve the impossible can be a frightening power if not controlled or used for positive outcomes. The emotion of fear itself becomes a significant self-limiting feature that, although often useful, also functions as a saboteur.

10

Fear: Dragon Guarding Our Treasures

Your power ends where your fear begins.

Barbara Marciniak, *Family of Light*

Just as mythical dragons guard great treasures, fear guards the entrance to our vast resources of power. Fear forms the basis for virtually all the ways we limit ourselves. It has been an ongoing project for me to recognize as many fear programs as possible, so I can make good decisions about how to manage them.

No doubt healthy fear protects us, and we need it to survive. Some limits are healthy. For that reason, fear is what we might call a core program, with an entire suite of brain/body mechanisms to support it. Because it functions continuously and automatically as a core program, it can be used to manipulate us below our level of awareness. While we each have to do our own detection work, we can set forth some working principles about fear programs and look at a few of the most common ways they manifest.

Our primal survival fear worked well in ancient times to protect us, but now it is triggered and manipulated constantly by modern life. In fact, the fear triggers never really stop firing. They are set off by almost every aspect of life: education, economics, work, and even entertainment including television programming, popular music, popular fiction, movies, journalism, and even news and weather reporting.

We live in a constant state of adrenalized fear-based motivation, which for many people has been a way of life for so long that they don't even realize it. Although this is a book-length topic in itself, I want to share some examples to provide you with clues to sharpen your own awareness of this phenomenon. It behooves each of us to know how these programs are manipulating us daily, and who might be using this for economic gain.

A first step in handling or reprogramming fear is to detect what triggers it.

As fast as you can, name one thing you are afraid of. What did you say? I would bet it had to do with losing something crucial to survival. It might be the fear of losing your income, job, home, your family, or your health. The fear of aging is related to all these primal fears. We fear loss of safety and loss of control over our life.

Now, think about the content of the advertising, entertainment, and reporting we are surrounded with every day. Ads about losing your health are juxtaposed with ads for products that can no doubt help you lose it, and then the services and products to help you re-gain it! Ads about help for your financial problems abound, following ads that entice you to spend money to get further in debt. Every other television advertisement sells advice on how to avoid foreclosure or safely navigate bankruptcy. Survival fear manipulation is rampant, and even if you do not think it is affecting you, it may be doing so below your level of awareness.

Media fear programs use symbolic forms, especially language, images, and sound or music, to trigger our emotions. For example, insurance is marketed based on fear of future loss, of health, of belongings, and of life itself. Health insurance makes use of evocative imagery and language, creating scenarios in which you could be terminally or seriously ill. Other insurance ads show car wrecks or home burglaries taking place, complete with scary sounds or dramatic music. One ad for life insurance that pops up on a popular web browser depicts a beautiful sad young girl dressed in black, laying flowers on a casket.

Most of the fear-based programs to which we respond daily can only do harm, so it behooves us to detect and "uninstall" them or desensitize ourselves so that we do not automatically react with negative thoughts, emotions, or behaviors. One of my all-time favorite books on this topic is entitled *Feel the Fear and Do It Anyway* by Susan Jeffers. Jeffers also reviews fear as our main power buster, stating that our main fear is the fear that we cannot handle our fears! She reminds readers that "whether you feel like it or not, you already have more power than you could ever have imagined....Inside of you, just waiting to emerge, is an incredible source of energy...."[1]

Jacob Liberman discusses the effects of fear at length, especially its effect of contracting or collapsing a person's visual and conceptual field. He concludes that "it seems that the underlying cause of most vision problems is a chronically collapsed field of awareness—a *fear of life*."[2] Like Jeffers's advice to work through the fears, Liberman suggests we respect and work through our fearful challenges as a form of what he calls "human homeopathy," where we are continuously faced with our greatest fears until we deal with them. This creates a life curriculum in "what you resist, persists."[3]

I find it helps to do some kind of scan and delete activity during a daily routine to get rid of the fear messages I may have absorbed that day without realizing it. I have success with a general affirmation that goes something like: "I now lovingly command that any fear programs that have been activated in me today by any means, internal or external, be resolved and deleted immediately." I check to see if there is any specific image, message, or behavior that seems to be triggering a fear response. As Susan Jeffers points out, the root of all fear is less about the fear focus event—death or poverty, for example—than it is about not being able to handle that event.

One of our greatest fears may be the fear of our own power.

We are often most afraid that we cannot handle our own power. Fear triggers avoidance (flight) as well as attack (fight), so one place I look for fear sabotage behavior is to notice what I am doing to avoid doing something else. Ironically, the fear traps which lure us away from our real power may look very much like new, exciting, or creative endeavors. These activities provide *false power.* They steal the juice of our real power while pretending to be forms of power.

False power activities seem to be just the ticket when we are afraid to discover our own power by doing any new and uncomfortable activity. Fear of using our own creative power, of making a mistake or failing, can delay or paralyze us for years while we wait for the "right time." Jeffers calls this the "when/then" game.[4] We dodge frightening opportunities for discovery by putting them off, saying, "When X happens, then I'll be ready to do Y."

Meanwhile, a long list of false power activities can seem to satisfy our needs: shopping, eating, drinking, reading, exercise, sex, surfing the Internet, taking courses, and many others. The list is as endless as the aspects of our power that they mirror. It is ironic that even the study of our human potential can become a form of false power; it may stand in for practice *using* our *actual* abilities. As I know well, people who want to be authors are often avid readers. Reading provides the mental exercise we crave and allows us to vicariously experience writing, but keeps us from our own creative work and our fears about it. I first discovered this while writing my dissertation. The urge to know more and more—and to be certain my thesis was original— kept me from getting the creation out into the world. Similar things happened as I moved forward with this book.

The good news is that false power activities do mirror the keys to our power areas. Think for a moment of any activity that feels creative and exciting to you, and that is something you use as a "go to" when you need to feel good. Two features let you know it is a false power activity: 1.) It takes more energy (or time or money) from you in the long run than it gives in the short run, and 2.) It does not result in a creation that is yours, it uses someone else's creation as a stand-in. Usually this activity profits someone else as well.

Just like the well-known symbol for yin and yang, we embody both dark and light. Our fears can be viewed as a part of the dark-side energies so integral to our human experience and power. Our ever-present underworld of fears has been represented throughout the ages by a variety of archetypes and symbols. In the Renaissance, this underworld was often represented by an iconic emblem bearing the Latin phrase, "*Et in Arcadia, ego*," which can be translated as "Also in Arcadia, here am I." The "I" was the dark side, evil, ugliness, and fear.

Arcadia was a Renaissance artistic convention. It represented the pastoral paradise, a place where happy shepherds tended sheep in a world of beauty, peace, harmony, safety, and timelessness. The emblem also depicted the fearful side of life that cannot be escaped -

demons and darkness lurking in rivers just below the surface of the happy Arcadia. The troublesome "ego" underneath Arcadia housed whatever we might fear, including, of course, the dark side of our power.

Although we may not often see the Arcadian emblem, we still control our scary emotions and thoughts by housing them underground, framing, limiting, or separating them from our daily experience. We also still use art – graphic arts, music, films and TV – to safely frame and experience the darker side of ourselves. Techniques of separation help us to limit and control emotional or mental phenomenon we cannot process comfortably. As we know, however, a great deal of positive power is guarded by our fear. Our openness to understand fear and be able to see beyond the dragons allows us better access to our true power.

11

Divide and Conquer: How Separation Weakens Us

In order to break free, in order to have a new experience, a shamanic awakening, a new vision, we must break free of the illusion that we are separate from anything else.

Fred Alan Wolf, *Mind Into Matter*

Fred Alan Wolf's words introduce key perspectives from which to re-view the nature and risks of what we call separation. If we believe that everything is energy or consciousness, then separation is an illusion because we are all part of one limitless construct. However, just as fear protects us from real danger, separation is an illusion necessary to much of everyday life. The problem comes when separation becomes a way of thinking that cuts us off from powerful resources within ourselves, others, or all of consciousness. When this happens, separation weakens us and blocks our ability to discover new worlds.

Awareness and balance seem to be the key to using separation in healthy ways. Maintaining too much separation in our physical, mental and emotional lives can allow this otherwise helpful illusion to "divide and conquer" us. That happens when instead of working with an awareness of our unity we function as so many thousands or millions of disparate entities, separated by belief systems and economic, political and cultural machines that pit us against each other. Awakening from this illusion would create a true re-birth of our species.

Separation functions in a positive way as a primary natural device we use to perceive ourselves and the world around us. Our physical bodies certainly seem to be separate and individual. Further, we create lots of positive, personal frames for our lives—our homes, our offices, our vehicles all separate us, but also house us, allowing us to express our individual personalities. We enjoy creating frames for reality, like windows that offer focus and perspectives. Framing can be seen as an important tool that enhances life.[5]

Conceptual separation or framing helps us to learn things. We are trained to learn about the world by separating ideas and items into categories or by creating outlines, diagrams, protocols, and formulas. Our analytical brain can then relate items by linking the separate frames, often forming systems of organization. This keeps reality orderly for us. For example, to create this book, I had to devise and use the best logical organization system I could to facilitate understanding. To explain the human renaissance view for readers, I had to separate and explain many concepts that I knew really functioned as one holistic construct—like the body/mind. In cases like this we rely on separation as a tool.

Separation begins to divide and weaken us when it functions as judgments and judgment systems, long-standing and accepted frames that artificially separate us based upon beliefs and values. We probably engage so easily in separation and judgment because our left-brain function always prefers to codify things and file them neatly. When we codify, however, we create conceptual boxes that can become rigid. When this happens, we have created a sort of mental prison, which limits our ability to see or think in new ways.

We have seen that when many people hold any belief or belief system over time, a strong morphic field forms that perpetuates itself within that matrix. This sturdy consensus field acts as a mental filter, making it difficult or impossible for people within any well-formed belief system to see another perspective.

Mental separators block our ability to see, keeping a huge new world of options invisible.

There is an anonymous saying that always comes to me when I observe rigidly codified belief systems. The saying goes: "Christ was not a Christian, nor Aristotle an Aristotelian." It is easy to forget that we, humans, codify belief systems over time. With each teacher or scholar or commentator we add new rules to create "*-isms*" that we then allow to define our world. No matter who the original teacher was, or how great, they likely would not recognize their own teachings and lives after years of human interpretation, translation, and codification. The doctrines attributed to them take on a life of their own. Even our great avatars and masters can become symbolic data manipulated by people and used as weapons of judgment, separating and weakening us.

Judgment programs rely on binary logic (much like computer language)—there is good and bad, right and wrong, "My way or the highway," or my favorite, "I like it/I don't like it." I learned a lot about this by teaching English composition for many years, where we taught mostly essay-writing skills. I used to deliver a lesson on how to move beyond binary thought and into discovery. Although many instructors taught some form of a five-paragraph essay with beginning, middle, and end, in my class students learned to use the essay to explore a topic. To use the essay this way is closer to the intention of the form's first master, Renaissance author Michel de Montaigne (1533-1592). In French, the verb "essayer" means "to try." So the essay seeks to try out ideas, not pin them to the wall like dead butterflies.[6]

My exploratory teaching experiment was fraught with danger. It produced some of the worst and some of the most brilliant student writing I had ever read. The experiment helped me demonstrate the ways that binary thinking shuts down our power to explore, to think broadly and deeply, and to generate new ideas. The principles also came in handy later when I was teaching communication in the workplace. The ability to think on your feet, so sought after in the world of work, is learned by practicing this type of exercise of free and expansive thought. Knowing that you can think outside the box and develop new ideas provides confidence and flexibility that rote formulas can never produce. In many ways, this has always been the point of the true liberal arts curriculum, often neglected in the late twentieth century.

Training in broad and curious thinking helps to establish a lifelong ability to expand beyond separation and judgment; this is the first step to seeing and creating new worlds. However, such training still encounters pushback from the consensus models that support a more binary thought process. Binary thinking is the way we are taught to operate in the world; we believe things must be either this way OR that way, right OR wrong.

Unfortunately the binary model always fails when situational flexibility is needed. Hard and fast beliefs or judgments are also not so durable. The old saying goes, "never say never," because experience shows that as we discover new things, our ideas about the old ones shift and change. Thus, a friend of mine who was "never going to cut my hair— never happening," months later was thrilled when someone talked her into doing it. She raved about how good she looked, what a great idea this was—completely forgetting her previous absolute declaration. She was ready to expand her view.

In decades of helping professionals achieve better interpersonal communication outcomes, I have dealt with an exhaustive array of fear, separation, and judgment programs in addition to just plain old binary thinking. Well-worn paths of cultural separation and judgment often lead to interpersonal dysfunctions. My job is to help clients see beyond the walls and filters that cause these organizational dilemmas. We help dismantle the constructs of separation by giving people a new view of the many different personality types and behavior styles that exist. Clients can begin to see the world through another's eyes, understand another's difference, and shift their own behaviors accordingly. Clients learn to move beyond their separateness, but also to value the idea that there are many individual viewpoints.

One huge benefit of enhanced interpersonal awareness is the realization that although it is tempting to react to one's own discomfort by judging another person, it is seldom productive. Most importantly, it is usually not true. Any person's interpretation of another's behavior is driven more by consciousness filters in the observer than by the actions or intentions of the one being observed.

I learned this very clearly when I first came to live in Miami. Fresh from the polite and friendly Midwestern culture, I was very uncomfortable most of the time with how I was being treated by others. No one spoke on the street or even looked at me and smiled.

If I smiled at them, they scowled at me even harder. They were also loud and seemed abrupt and rude, when they were not being aloof. They were pushy and extremely selfish, I judged. It was all about them; no sharing or caring. These others also had no idea how to drive. Their behavior made driving in traffic a nightmare—no rules were followed at all, and there was no courtesy.

Eventually, I learned that most of this behavior was based on cultural diversity. I live in a place of diversity, plus we have a constant flow of tourists from everywhere. People have a wide variety of communication styles and attitudes, and as for the driving, some places in our world have few or NO driving rules at all. When I arrive back to Miami from a trip and the first airport taxi-stand guy seems rude to me, or the first driver cuts in front of me to make a left turn from the right lane, I say to myself, "Welcome home!"

Just as it took me a few years to figure out what was happening in Miami, I have found that in any interpersonal situation, the longer I can delay judgment to see what might really be going on with someone else, the better the outcome will be. I have to wait until I can see better! "Wait and see" has become a sort of mantra with me.

Although we have made huge strides in shifting cultural, racial, gender, religious, and other types of judgment programs, the whole construct presents a challenge. The power of language becomes important here as well. The label of "diversity" ironically carries its own power to polarize and separate, which I am sure many of us notice. It is as if we invoke the effect of separation (diversity) in the name of creating unity. This sets up an inherent opposition and tension that we all feel. Most of us can think of at least one experience where being part of some labeled diversity group—like women or minority business owners—has created an "us versus them" situation, defeating the original intention. What we really wanted was NOT to be perceived and treated as different. If we realize this, our expanded awareness can help us create positive outcomes instead of negative ones.

For example, as a female in the traditionally male business world, I have often found myself in situations where I wondered if I was being treated unfairly or differently because of my gender. I learned to question my own filters, and to ask myself if I had interpreted someone's behavior from my own beliefs about gender prejudice.

Did that person really say what I heard, or did I interpret their words according to my own filters?

I often took such issues to male friends and asked their perspective. Of course, many times they just told me to forget about it—that men say things all the time that have no hidden meaning. I also read up on the differences that do exist in the ways men and women think and process the world, so I could have awareness of the male perspective. It helped a lot for me to understand male business behavior as a cultural phenomenon, and develop a new set of filters just for those situations.

Most importantly, I realized that my own judgments about others (in this case, men) were certainly not helping *me* to achieve happiness. Even in situations involving unacceptable behavior based on gender bias, it was still up to me to release the negative emotions caused by the events. In the end, I could only control myself. If I could take an issue less personally, a positive outcome was more likely, at least for me. Actually I have found that by taking things less personally and asking to understand another's remarks or behavior, the whole energy of a difficult situation can change, and we both learn something. Like using the sonic screwdriver, it just shifts that polarity and drops the tension.

To discover our new world we need techniques to re-move our many invisible barriers.

Our challenges remain because separation is woven deeply into our lives. Our renaissance success will be enhanced by our individual and collective willingness to be more self-aware, explore without judgment, and endure some uncomfortable challenges to the way it's always been. Think of what might be possible if we used unity-consciousness to tap into and positively harness the shared power of millions or even billions of people.

I-solation: Personal World as Separator

Ironically, although technology affords us instant access to each other, we are becoming more and more separated as human beings. A critical trend toward separation in our society can be seen in the growing number of ways that people can distance themselves from each other while seeming to be super-connected. Almost everyone has several personal communication and computing devices, and most of these are portable. We use these to "connect" with people we may never know personally through the growing number of social media vehicles we can access through the Internet.

Although technology can foster better and wider connections, it can also promote self-referential and disconnected mental habits and behaviors. In many ways, today's many media act as vehicles for non-stop self-promotion and continuous competition in a new sort of everyday people's marketplace.

A friend of mine has called our time "the age of rampant narcissism." We might also call this phenomenon "I-solation." Our current world of over-connectedness may have triggered this phenomenon, but it also feeds on it. I-solation consciousness and the many cultural and media systems that support it represent an enormous commercial enterprise. Once again, divide and conquer is profitable.

As we have seen in our review of separation, I-solation in its basic form has always been present. Our self-worlds are necessary to the extent that they allow us to be self-aware, to develop, mature and care for ourselves. Challenges come when we must flex our I-world boundaries to understand and interact with another person. It can be a shock to realize another person can have starkly different reality from ours. Not only might they have a different belief, they may see an entirely opposite "reality" from the one we think is real.

In my early twenties, I had a memorable experience that taught me about this concept. As a part-time job in college, I sold wigs at a mall retailer. One day, a woman with salt-and-pepper gray hair came into the shop. She declared that she wanted a wig to match her hair. No problem. I cheerily sat her down and plucked a perfect match from the wig display tree. As I went to place it on her head, she began to screech, "No, no that's not my color! Get it away!" She was very distraught—pushing my hand away forcefully.

I scrambled to use what skills I could remember from psychology about dealing with difficult people. Immediately removing the wig and putting it in a drawer, I very calmly said, "Oh, I am so sorry. I made a mistake and just grabbed that one. To be sure I get it right, can you show me your color here on the display?" She chose a very dark brown wig, almost black. I concealed my horror and did my best to get it on her so the gray would not show.

She loved it. Although the front looked totally phony and the color was not a match with her skin, she was so happy. She was now the girl she used to be and wanted to be once again. "You see?" she exclaimed. "It's a perfect match." "Oh, yes," I replied. She paid for it happily and wore it out of the store. Although I was slightly embarrassed for her, she was happy. She might be able to accept her gray hair later, or not, but the black wig filled an important need for her. Her inner and outer worlds did not match, and she needed to make that happen when it was right for her. Meanwhile, the wig allowed her to re-create the look essential to her idea of herself and of her youth.

It was clear to me that the customer and I saw two very different realities when we looked at her. Just as I was amazed that I could not really see the enormity of the Grand Canyon, I was amazed there could be two such different versions of this woman, but that's how it was. I could only help the woman by trying my best to see with her eyes. I was sure what I saw was the truth – she looked horrid in that black wig. But what she saw was a beautiful young woman. To make this point in workplace coaching and training, we often use one of the many silhouette pictures that represent two very different images depending on the viewer's orientation. In one, a person can see either a beautiful woman or an old hag – just like my wig experience. Both pictures are true, because there are two truths!

Reducing I-solation creates better interpersonal results and expands personal freedom.

The extreme stresses of today's world combine with our normal tendencies toward self-reference to create situations where we rely on technology at the expense of natural relationships that can support our health. We can also become extra vulnerable to power-weakening programming through our constant exposure to media and its host of commercial products. It becomes easy to live in a false world, a replication that depicts our flesh-and-blood world, but is not.

Our technology makes this possible and reminds me of the *Star Trek* holodeck, where one could go to have a life-like experience with holograms that were simulations of real people, places and events. The Enterprise crew's holodeck adventures are not so different from our experience with today's advanced technologies. Video games and other computer simulations, and high definition TV, have the ability to simulate much of the sensory experience of people, nature, places and events. The energy of the natural world, with all its power to convey information and health, cannot be fully experienced second or third-hand. Nevertheless, our increasing dependence on technological environments promotes this type of replicated interaction, and perpetuates I-solation.

Consensus reality supports and strengthens I-solation through our growing dependence on personal communication devices. On a trip to the supermarket the other day, I almost ran into more than eight folks of all ages who had ear buds or headphones attached and were looking at their phones instead of their surroundings, while in the midst of some pretty intense vehicular and pedestrian traffic.

EXERCISE:

This exercise has three steps. The first is a warm up to open awareness to I-solation behaviors. The second is the application of that new awareness to you. The third step is creating and implementing changes to your own behaviors.

Step One: Focus on Them. The first step focuses on the other person because it is always easier to see behaviors in someone else, even though their behavior acts as a mirror for us.

1. **Pick a colleague or friend** you speak with regularly. In your next conversation, see if you can jot down or mentally **count how many times they begin a sentence with the first person singular pronoun "I."**
2. **Tell the other person about something** interesting you have read or seen or something you have experienced or learned. You might want to ask for advice. Keep it short (smile).
3. Then **see how they respond to you.** Do they ask you questions or seem to be actively listening to you, or do they immediately compare your experience to one of theirs and then expound on their story? Notice if they talk over you

when you are talking, or do other self-centered behaviors that indicate they are not paying attention to you or giving you equal time.

4. **Record or list the behaviors that you noticed.**

Focusing on others at first allows us to see how the invisible I-solation programs work, so we can detect them in ourselves.

Step Two: Focus on You. The next step switches the focus to you, applying what you learned in step one. To do your own detection, pick one day and notice your own behaviors just as you did in the exercises above. You can use your list from the previous observation and check your own conversation or even your thoughts. Here's a starter list:

1. Choose several conversations with others during your day, and **notice how many times you talk just about yourself or start sentences with the pronoun "I."** What percentage of the conversation do you lead with your stories or thoughts?
2. **When someone tells you something about themselves, how do you react**? Do you listen with focus on them and maybe ask for more details? Do you respond with a story about you?
3. **Monitor your thoughts and feelings as someone speaks to you**. Are they triggering you to feel competitive or like you have to keep up? Can you remain neutral while you listen, or actually put yourself in their place, or do you stay in your I-world?
4. Do you **interrupt people or talk over them**? Do you **monopolize** conversations?
5. Is the **other person signaling you** that you are monopolizing the conversation? Listen for phrases such as "uh-huh" or phrases that indicate they are trying to end the interaction. In person, you can check for body language such as fidgeting, loss of eye contact, or shifting body positions.
6. After your day, **make your own list.** What behaviors will be easiest to tackle first? Pick one you'd like to change.

Step Three: Change Something. This step uses the Just One Thing technique we have already reviewed. Let's say you are aware that you talk too much about yourself and don't really listen to the other person. To practice what is called "active listening," do the following:

1. **Show the person that you are listening** to them by making eye contact and nodding if in person, and by occasionally showing that you hear them by saying short phrases like, "I hear you," or "I see."
2. **Resist the urge to interrupt or to talk about yourself.**
3. **Reflect back to the person what they have said** at appropriate points to show them you are hearing them. For example you can say "So, Sue, what I hear you saying is that..." or "That sounded like an interesting experience. You did such and such, right?"
4. If you are asked for advice, **focus on the other person's situation** and refer to their options or ideas without comparing them to yours. You may also want to ask clarifying questions, probing for more information and letting them know you hear them. If you do use your own experience to demonstrate a point or idea, let them know that you realize their situation is unique and that you are using your perspective to assist *them.*

Although these types of remedies may seem trite, they get results. If more people actually practiced them we'd have a better connected human world. Doing what we can to address the challenges of I-solation benefits us all as we work toward re-discovering ourselves and seeing things from new perspectives.

12
The Almighty Time Program

Dynamic Duo: Time and Aging

But at my back I always hear
Time's winged chariot hurrying near.
And yonder all before us lie
Deserts of vast eternity.

Andrew Marvell, *To His Coy Mistress*

Marvell's famous image conveys our age-old reaction to the inescapable "reality" of time and death, as the ever-present "winged chariot" of time chases us down into the unknown, fearful "deserts of vast eternity." If those deserts were just about death, it might not affect us so deeply, but our minds cannot take us out of life without the specter of aging. Time and aging act as a dynamic duo which invisibly controls most of our experience of life.

As with all of our invisible drivers, enhanced awareness creates our first movement. Re-viewing both of these important consciousness phenomena can be a giant step toward creating a new reality.

Time as a Program

Believe it or not, time is a frequency, and a frequency is not measurable by a clock. It is the nature of time to synchronize all things and to maintain all things in a condition of synchronization. Synchronicity, then, is the experience of real time.

Jose Arguelles, *Time and the Technosphere*

Even though some cultures on our planet do not place any value on clock time, it governs most of what we believe to be civilized life. No matter how it functions in the cultural system, though, time constitutes a huge consensus reality program. Of course, time itself is totally invisible, and as Jose Arguelles points out, "real" time may be more a frequency and a flow. Under that definition, time is an organic ordering system that cannot be reduced to, or depicted by, a machine like a clock.

If you asked someone to actually show you time, what would they do? They might point to a clock, but the clock simply represents our sequential time system. They might reference the natural cycle—day and night, the seasons or phases of the moon. But these cycles are not linear and often cause us to have to adjust clock time. Clocks are a symbolic representation of our mass beliefs about how time functions. As such, they are useful when we have to operate successfully in the consensus world that created clock time and uses it to structure life.

I don't know about you, but in my family, clock time ruled our lives. Time governed all activities, and we were rewarded or punished for our ability to be "punctual" (that word even feels like a "puncture" to me). Because of the rigidity of the time program in my family, I started early to find ways to "beat the clock," so I have done a lot of exploring in the frontier of time. As a child, I talked with my invisible guides about past, present, and future being simultaneous. They repeatedly told me that only earth had time, and it was basically a very plastic construct you could manipulate, or experience in a more expanded way.

Although many people have experienced time as fluid or plastic, most of us choose to use regular consensus clock time, because it structures our everyday life. Nevertheless, we have always demonstrated an interest in exploring the frontier of time. We like the idea of being able to "make time stand still" or "go back in time," or "travel to the future," and we have many stories, movies, and myths about time travel of various sorts. In short, we have been questioning time since "the beginning of time," whenever that was.

A glance back at literature, music, or art reveals our continuing fascination with and resistance to clock time. In the historical Renaissance, poets like Andrew Marvell, John Donne, Ben Jonson, and Shakespeare drew on classical models to create works either bemoaning the fact of time in *carpe diem* poems or songs, or escaping it through various art genres, including elaborate masques, plays (which brought live fiction to real people), and many almost surreal graphic art forms. Fiction always suspends time and space and creates its own world of entertainment, and Renaissance artists were extremely aware of this artistic ethos.

Each era has had its representations of the time/no time themes and imagines what devices might allow us to manipulate time/space. In the twentieth century, my sci-fi hero Doctor Who traveled the cosmos in a device called a TARDIS, an acronym for "time and relative dimension in space." The TARDIS also included a quantum non-linear spatial or dimensional feature, because no time and no space make a good quantum pair. Those of you who have followed *Doctor Who* know that his machine malfunctioned quite a bit, sending its own message about our beliefs regarding time. As we moved into the twenty-first century, movies like *What the Bleep Do We Know* (2001), based on principles of quantum physics, have acted as message boards about our growing awareness of the plasticity of time.

Most people have been altering time all their lives, often without knowing it.

Ask anyone you know, or ask yourself, if you have ever had an experience where time stood still, sped up, or slowed down. Of course you have! If time were absolute, that could not have happened. Among the many ways we regularly alter or suspend time, one of the most common is our creation and enjoyment of recreational frames like theatres, concert halls, and sports venues. We create controlled enclosures for experiences that alter or temporarily replace the real time world. In these special venues, we engage completely in the created world of an event, a world with its own time or no-time.

A. Bartlett Giamatti's insightful work entitled *Take Time for Paradise,* discusses this idea in detail, as he describes baseball and other American sports as ways we re-create paradise. Giamatti calls attention also to our word "recreation," pointing out that in fact, any form of recreation is a "re-creation."[7] And like our renaissance, these re-creations take place in contexts where we allow ourselves new perspectives, including a different experience of time. Meditation is another increasingly popular technique for altering our experience of both time and space.[8]

Time, as we are trained to experience it, is what we might call a master program. It is used or is involved in almost everything we do, and in the way we think about who we are. I do not propose we do away with time! I propose we take a renaissance re-view of time to reclaim our power to engage it as a tool and not a limitation.

Creating a Time Envelope Tool

My studies in alternative ways of knowing the world led me to meditate actively with the intention to experience time differently. I decided to create what I came to call a "time envelope." The time envelope is an intentional suspension of dynamic sequential time, so you can go to places or do things without the worry of having enough time. No worry, no rush—you are just in the flow. Trust and intention govern your experience of time, aligning you with synchronicity.

The time envelope works by getting *inside* of time, not outside of it.

I decided that by embracing and entering the flow of natural time, I could avoid polarity problems, so I could create the conditions for synchronicity. To create the conditions for this, I affirmed my own version of time as a fluid field, not governed by clocks. Then I visualized myself easing into the flow of that time field, and being present in the fluidity of its invisible flow. Before I entered the flow, I simply needed to state what time I would arrive at the destination, "set it and forget it." Then I would just enjoy the ride. My first experiments took place in my car, when I had to be somewhere at a specific time.

Because clocks support and maintain our consensus time program, the first order of business is not to look at a clock during an experiment. In my car, I kept a Band-Aid over the digital clock. This worked great. Let's say I had a 10:00 a.m. appointment at my office in downtown Chicago, and it normally took about twenty-five minutes to drive to the office from my house and park. I would practice leaving the house at different clock times that allowed me less than the normal time. I looked only once at the clock to check when I left, but not again until I arrived. I would announce my intention as I got into the car: "I arrive at my office at exactly 10:00."

When I kept my focus open, let all worry about time simply pass away, and kept the Band-Aid firmly affixed to the clock, my experiments were about 60 percent successful at first. Although I did not tell too many people about my time envelope, I did share it with one New Age teacher who surprised me when she responded, "This is excellent! Learning to work with time is one of the first steps to mastery. You are on your path. Keep going." Her support cheered me, although I still felt pretty much on my own, as I had no guidebook that specifically addressed working with everyday time. In fact, until that teacher congratulated me, no one had ever taught me anything about actually working with time.

My greatest confirmation of the effectiveness of my time envelope came one January evening as I set out to attend a lecture by a well-known spiritual master. I had been encouraged to go to this introductory lecture and to attend the master's workshops over the following weeks. I had a lot on my plate and was ambivalent about going. I am also anti-guru by nature and had a built-in distrust of people called "masters," since they seemed to be everywhere in the New Age, and their credentials often seemed questionable. All throughout the day of the lecture, I battled with myself about going or not going. I put off the decision until the very last minute.

The lecture was scheduled for 7:00 p.m. in a chapel at a university about a half hour away from my house by car. The day was cold and blustery. As night fell, it began to snow and temperatures plummeted into the 20s with a strong wind chill. I really did not want to go. I went to the gym and dawdled through my routine, drove slowly home through the snow, and grudgingly showered and dressed to go. Looking at the clock on the way out the door, I remarked, "Well, universe—here's the test! If I am really supposed to meet this guy, let's get me there at 7:00!" All my clocks read 6:45.

I did my time envelope practice: staying in the moment, Band-Aid on clock, driving carefully—smooth, not fast. Every possible obstacle and delay occurred. I hit all the red lights; the snow kept coming down on top of a layer of ice. Dogs, children, old ladies, bad drivers—you name it—all came into my path. Finally, I got to the campus and had to find parking. I also did not know the exact location of the chapel where the lecture was to be held.

Finally I parked, got directions from passing students, and walked in mounting snow for about four blocks into the campus. At last I spotted the brightly lit chapel. It was packed—standing room only—as I entered. I looked over the sea of people, and to my surprise, there was a woman in a row about halfway down and center, waving excitedly at me and pointing to an empty seat. There was a huge group of people around me looking for seats, but it was as if they disappeared for one very calm moment, and there she was, focusing just on me. I had never seen this woman before in my life. I walked down the aisle, then excused my way into the empty seat. This was no time to argue with synchronicity.

"Hi," she chirped, "I'm Alice!" "Hi, Alice," I said, "thanks for the seat." "Of course!" she replied. Since I had some experience meeting unknown people who were apparently sent to help me, I just smiled and patted her arm. Then I thought about the time. "Say, Alice, can you tell me what time it is now?" I inquired. "Why, yes," she replied, "it's just 7:00." Just then the lights went down and the program began. I said a silent prayer of gratitude. Even though I challenged the envelope, it still worked. I truly was supposed to be there, and all synchronicity supported me.

Once I became confident using the time envelope, I found it useful in many situations. I also found that I seemed to be running a sort of parallel monitoring system for clock time, so I always knew what time it was. I was learning to shift between the worlds of clock and synchronous time. I stopped wearing a watch, and I am still usually on time for clock time appointments, unless I start worrying about it.

Years after starting to use my time envelope, I was pleasantly surprised to read Jose Arguelles' declaration that "time itself, well, believe it or not, time is a frequency, and a frequency is not measurable by a clock. The Law of Time states that time is the universal frequency of synchronization. It is the nature of time to synchronize and to maintain all things in a condition of synchronization. Synchronicity, then, is the experience of real time."[9]

Later, I would be even happier when Gregg Braden, in his book *Fractal Time,* also explained that the "code" of "real" time was a cyclical phenomenon more related to a fractal-like endless repetition of "conditions."[10] As our renaissance progresses, we are discovering a new world of time. From my own experience, I can say that this new world really exists, and perhaps more importantly, it can co-exist with the world of consensus clock time.

Time Envelope Guidelines

When you try the time envelope, please remember that because time functions as a major life-organizing system or program, it remains stubborn. So if you do not feel like Doctor Who right away—or maybe if you do—keep going. Some days you may fail to get inside the envelope. That's OK, there's always more time.

When you begin to explore the world of no time, the first principle is—no clocks! It means that to really get into this frontier, you should leave your watch in the drawer, place clocks where you cannot see them (or cover up displays), and put a Band-Aid or something over any digital clock display. In short, wherever you will perform your experiment, *do not look at the clock.*

You will decide when to do your experiments, but I like to do them on days when I am not under much stress. Stressful situations will send you flying back to your old default programs, so it is best to start when you are pretty relaxed. Just choose any task or a trip you would like to use for practice.

Exercise:

A time envelope experiment involves the following basic steps:

1. **Choose your task or event**—for example, a trip to the store. Note how long that usually takes in clock time, let's say fifteen minutes from your house to the store, door to door.

2. **Pick a time you would like to arrive** at the store. Make it somewhat reasonable when you begin. For example, if you think it should take fifteen minutes, decide you will arrive in ten or maybe eight minutes.
3. **Look at a clock only once**—when you set out—to get your start time, then affirm: "I will be at the store at 10:00." Then leave.
4. **After that, do not look at any clocks** or listen to a radio station or anything that might tell you the clock time, until you arrive. Remember, "set it and forget it."
5. While travelling, **stay in the zone by keeping your focus only on the present**. Tell yourself that there is only **one huge expanded now** and you are inside of it, like a big lovely cocoon or envelope. You are in a flow that is always there and has its own wisdom. Your timely arrival is assured. Don't meddle.
6. **Stay physically, mentally, and emotionally relaxed and open**. If you feel anxious, tight, fidgety, or your mind begins chattering about being late, breathe deeply and focus on something totally different. I find it helps to chatter to myself out loud about silly stuff I notice along the way—a sign, a building, a dog, someone's shoes—anything to distract the mind. You might want to think about a favorite vacation place or eating a special food, whatever will take your worry-wart mind away from time.
7. **Resist any urge to rush.** In fact, do the opposite, no matter what happens. Your mantra is "smooth beats fast." You are gliding through the world on a sort of smooth carpet of energy. You are aware of all that is around you and are flowing with it perfectly. No matter what happens, it's okay because you are in a programmed flow, and you have already set it for the 10:00 result. You have already arrived at the set time. *You are meeting yourself there.*
8. **Remember: If you RESIST time, it will PERSIST.**
9. **Have fun!** Fun relaxes you, so it is easier to stay in the zone.

As you near your destination, it is imperative to keep in this flow. Stay open and in the now. Park your car carefully and slowly.

Walk in a relaxed way to the door of the store. **Once at your destination, check the time**, which you know already to be 10:00.

You can use the time envelope on any task or event—from cooking to work projects or any activity. If you are involving others in the activity, however, it may not work as well, unless they are willing to shift their consciousness, too. Remember, the time program is held in place and strengthened by the power of collective belief. But explore and have fun! I think you will be pleasantly surprised at how often you succeed.

Time Envelope Mantras

- **I am inside the wise, limitless, flowing envelope of time.**
- **My timely arrival is assured. I set it, now I can forget it.**
- **Smooth beats fast. I am on the smooth magic carpet of the now.**
- **This is fun!**

13
Aging: Ultimate Power Thief

Aging is a mistake.

Deepak Chopra, *Perfect Health*

Deepak Chopra may have been one of the first New Age authorities to fully address the topic of age, declaring, "Although everyone falls prey to the aging process, no one has ever proved that it is necessary."[11] My goal is to review major features of age belief programming, expand awareness, and explore some ways to shift our experience by shifting our beliefs. Maturing and dying are integral to our life process, but I believe we can do both with greater ease, beauty, and health. Our current aging program limits, destroys, and often bankrupts us, undermining our innate ability to remain vital and healthy until we die.

Just like the images in the *Et in Arcadia* emblems, the specter of death resides in our consciousness, whether we are aware of it or not. As our cultural programs work to keep us aware of the clock ticking, we become ultra sensitive to age. Our staunch mass beliefs about time inform our beliefs about stages of our life based on chronology. The aging program partners with clock time to manipulate and steal human power.

Aging in our culture represents a behemoth economic engine—an industry that preys effectively on almost all people. The lucrative and pervasive aging program has been running in most civilized human populations for hundreds, if not thousands, of years. Frankly, we do not know much about how really ancient people aged, because if you think about it, we do not see depictions of old, decrepit Mayans or Egyptians, nor do we read hieroglyphic accounts about taking Pharaoh to the nursing home. In fact, biblical stories often involve immense life spans like that of Methuselah at 969 years, Noah at 950, or even Abraham at 175. I think we can greatly expand the length and the quality of our lives.

Beliefs About Aging

Here is a re-view of some current consensus beliefs about aging.

1. **Aging is invisibly controlled by pre-installed and inalterable DNA** over which the individual human has no control—we just have to live with it.
2. **Aging is a degenerative process dictated by chronology.** The belief is that we begin to age after only a couple of decades. We do not describe children as "aging" but as "growing up" or "maturing." Our rather short span to maturity (birth to twenties) leads to what becomes known as "aging" by age thirty or even earlier. Then it is pretty much downhill.
3. **We all have an invisible "biological clock" that tells our bodies when to make certain degenerative changes** that are pre-set for manifestation during certain decades. For example, we learn to expect our near-vision eyesight to fail during our forties or fifties, causing us to need reading glasses, after which we expect various surgeries for cataracts, glaucoma, and so on. These pre-set changes form the marketing schedule for all the products and services of the aging industry.

   Products of all kinds, from vitamins to cosmetics, to prescription drugs and surgical procedures, are target-marketed to age groups. This is for "men over forty," or "women over fifty." Certain age numbers have become milestones for potential degeneration. I am sure you can think of many more examples.
4. **We lose power in all areas of our life as we age.** This belief especially affects the following:
   - **Work:** We lose the power to function effectively in the workplace, so we must "retire." Look at the many implications of that word. Although we have

altered the pre-set age number on that program feature a bit, the consensus reality still maintains its basic core idea: aging causes us to lose our power and thus our viability and value in the workforce. Older folks should "take it easy" and rest or travel, "now that they have time." Funny how we believe you actually get some time to use for yourself, but not until you've almost run out of it altogether.

- **Money:** Because we can no longer make money, we need to hoard lots of money to live on; hence, most of our viable working years are devoted to and focused on getting and investing, or stockpiling income-producing vehicles. The long-term goal is to "die with money," as a friend of mine says. We must also hoard lots of money to leave to our children, so they can get a head start on dying with money.
- **Sexual power:** Sex is one of our core power areas, so, of course, the aging industry targets sexual power for economic gain by creating expectations of various age-related difficulties. For men, this means erectile dysfunction or ED, which was virtually unheard of in the media until the past decade or so. Year by year, the men in the commercials get younger, and people are encouraged to begin buying drugs sooner to grow the market. For women, it is not only hormone replacement but also products for "loss of libido," or even surgeries for "vaginal rejuvenation."
- **Health and self-sufficiency:** As the aging process rolls out with its continuous degenerative shifts and loss of meaningful work and personal power, we become increasingly less self-sufficient and more dependent on outside care. This final segment of the process ushers in an overwhelming array of products and services, which by this time are often not optional.

The last decades of life often consist of a continuous series of doctor visits, prescription drugs, hospitalizations, and surgeries. As body parts wear out, decay, or break, they can be replaced by a stream of surgeries. Joints such as hips and knees are prime targets, as folks attempt to hang on to mobility, which is one of the scariest of the expected losses one suffers in the aging process. By the way, I do not suggest that joint replacement is wrong. Many people have recovered their lives that way. The crucial frontier is our *belief* that all our parts wear out and will need to be replaced because they cannot be renewed or kept healthy throughout life.

Using our power means understanding that we manifest what we expect. When we learn to govern our own expectations, our beliefs, we dramatically improve the quality of our lives.

If we change our beliefs about aging, how many age-related medical issues might disappear?

Ultimately, the process leads to the need for in-home helpers or incarceration in some sort of assisted or skilled care facility. Before death, the aging process can culminate in a complete inability to accomplish what has come to be known as "ADLs," short for activities of daily life. Increasing numbers of humans end up warehoused in skilled care facilities, unable to do almost anything. The big pile of money we have hoarded is crucial to support this final phase of disease and degeneration, which, under current conditions, can last for decades. The cost of long-term care in skilled facilities is staggering.

Once I began making my notes about aging beliefs, I was astounded at the breadth and depth of this consciousness system. As an exercise, take a day to note how many aging-related messages you take in. Notice the media messages—TV, radio, newspapers, billboards, emails, and Internet advertisements and pop-ups. Worse yet, pay attention to how many times in a day you hear yourself, or someone you know say things like, "Well, at our age," or "You have to expect that at our age," or "Things are different now than when were younger. We can't do that anymore."

It's also interesting to note how many times you find yourself (or hear someone else) asking first about a new person: "How old is she/he?" Once we have the magic age number for a person, we locate the programmatic pre-set age features, by which we then judge and define them. Of course, we are constantly defining ourselves by age, at conscious or unconscious levels. In addition to the consensus belief field we live in, our aging belief programs are supported and driven by the enormous media messaging machine. TV, radio, Internet, and all the media that assault us every day are working us over to sell products based on the aging belief system.

During the past decade or so, I have often chosen not to tell people my chronological age. I especially like to do this when a woman gives me the back-handed compliment, "You look so amazing for your age," then asks, "How old are you?" When I smile and say, "I don't do age," or "I don't like to energize that by talking about it," they really get miffed. Try it; the reactions are quite revealing about our self-definition through age.

My re-view is preliminary; I am sure you can add more examples of aging program beliefs and associated market features. The point is to become more aware of how aging functions as a mass consensus program. It is huge, deep, old, and well supported by the collective matrix. However, most of the matrix members would change the program if they thought they could. So next, we will look at ways we might begin to reprogram ourselves.

REPROGRAMMING AGING: MAYBE IT'S TIME

A renaissance seems the right time to explore real options to the consensus model of aging. Since the aging programs are so long-standing and so deep, we want to look at ways to begin shifting our beliefs and gently creating a new consciousness matrix about aging.

Here are some ideas I use in my own re-programming:

- **Decide not to participate fully in consensus aging**; do not resist it, just do not *be* an age.
    - Language note: a friend of mine notes that in French, one "has" an age instead of "being" an age. She comments, "Maybe that's why French women stay youthful for so long." Language represents belief and belief drives reality.
- **Detach from age as a way of thinking about, defining, or judging yourself or anyone else.** Be aware of yourself when you do ask how old people are, and try to stop before you ask. If others ask your age, don't answer, or you can lie.

Have fun with this. The exercise enhances awareness – a first step to re-programming.

- **Live in this moment** only and decide how you look/feel/ are right now in the power zone of the present.
- **Pick an age you like.** You are in control, so you can pick different ones depending on how you feel. You might even choose one age for your body, one for your overall public image, one for your sexuality, and so on. Deepak Chopra described this as setting our own "biostat."[12]
- **Consciously delete what I call "old contract" aging program messages** as they pop up, which they will. Do not resist them; just try to let them go. The basic premise is to acknowledge the old belief message. For example, "You can't read the menu because you are fifty." Let it go and replace it lovingly with your message—"I am able to read the menu perfectly because my eyes are optimal."
- **Get out the sonic screwdriver and shift the polarity of pushback to aging.** Work on expanding your power interfaces—your mind, your body, your emotions. Be flexible and open. The stronger you feel, the less likely you will be to fall back into old or undesirable programs.
- **Join a group matrix that supports your new worldview.** Be around more people who share your belief system. This will give your new programs a boost of collective power and will also strengthen your ability to be less affected by the old programs.

Aging is Big Business. The aging industry grows as Baby Boomers consume, and are consumed by it.

Ironically, many boomers who are degenerating along the new pre-set (anti) aging clock think they have shifted the program when, in fact, we have simply changed the pre-set ages. Even the language we use to describe youthfulness in later years gives this away, as we still USE chronology to define ourselves. For example, if we say, "Fifty is the new thirty," we did not change our belief, we just played with the numbers. The aging program is alive, well, and making money.

Because many of us have developed new beliefs about aging, we are experiencing new processes in our body/mind—what some New Age writers have called "ascension in the body." Although popular literature seems to have labeled this a 2012 phenomenon, I believe it actually may be the way our innate operating system is meant to function over time. Rather than undergoing a steady downhill slide, I believe the body continuously recycles and renews, even as it matures. Most people accept that our skin and many organs (like the liver) renew in regular cycles, so the idea that the whole body constantly renews is not such a stretch. The idea of this type of natural cycle or flow for aging aligns with a willingness to perceive and experience time in new ways that are more fluid and related to our own consciousness.

Our challenge, as it is with the entire time phenomenon, is to release old beliefs and be open to options for expansion—in this case, the option for our bodies to remain vital by periodically recycling throughout an indeterminate life span that could be over a hundred years or more. Death comes naturally to us, but when it does, we are not a physical, mental, and emotional ruin. I believe we can die aware and healthy.

New ways to age are part of a new world, so we have few guidelines, maps, or even language for understanding how this new aging phenomenon works. Like most discoveries, it reveals itself if we remain open and committed to it. I always try to remember that we are discovering what is already there. It is important to remember, though, that we can easily misinterpret what is happening to us if we use our old maps.

Instead, we can become aware of what's on those old maps and realize when we are following them, or we may lose opportunities to make important changes. This becomes critical when we begin the slippery slope to altering our bodies in keeping with the pre-set aging "cues" and protocols. Our current belief systems program us to expect and manifest certain "signs of aging," as we have already noted. The current program further dictates that once any of these signs appears, we must launch into a series of medical protocols. Once that happens, one may take actions, which might permanently alter our body's own innate programs and prevent our innate repair and re-form cycle to take effect.

When we begin the process of health-related activities that "older people need to do," we may trigger a downward spiraling health program. The course of this costly and unhealthy spiral can span decades. Ultimately, it involves increasing need for medication, surgeries, other forms of expensive care, possible admission to some level of care facility, and then death.

What if we treated "signs of aging" more like growing pains?

I am excited to explore ways to shift the aging program now that my own buttons are being pushed. In my forties and fifties, it was rather easy for me to change my physical form, appearance, and health to meet my intentions. The consensus reality of my generation supported my exploration and work staying young. It was fun and accepted, almost like a game. In the 1990s and 2000s, phrases like "forty (or fifty) is the new twenty" became popular as my group of Boomers launched our aging revolution. We took sex and rock'n'roll mainstream, why not aging?

I was somewhat surprised when my aging program triggers went off as I reached sixty. Several conditions contributed to this. One factor was my exposure to the intense morphic field of traditional aging as I spent more and more time with my parents in their world. I spent most of my fifties caring for sick and dying people who were following the old maps for aging and death. Even though I believed in alternatives to these consensus programs, my immersion in the field of my parents, aunts, and their peer group, began to affect my internal self-concept. As my old beliefs were rekindled, I saw and felt changes in my body/mind at all levels.

Another factor was that in my own age group, colleagues and friends were following the consensus aging maps and cues. People I liked and respected were off to the doctors to check everything all the time, getting this and that test or procedure—it had started. They were beginning to have surgeries, to alter their bodies. But I wasn't participating. Was I wrong? My trust in my own belief system began to falter, and when that happened, I began to see some of the consensus effects showing up in my body and my health. My own strong health programs began to "wobble." Underneath the surface of my alternative belief system was a recording saying that maybe it was true that the real downhill slide began in your sixties, when you should retire, travel and do all those things one does before you die. This chatter began to cause dissonance.

Adding to the challenge was my increasing emotional and mental vulnerability. During a decade dealing with severe illness and death, I came face to face with some of the toughest personal issues I had ever encountered. The loss of my parents and three close relatives in only a few years left me depressed and at sea. I had spent considerable energy, time, and money helping these family members through their transitions. While helping my family, I also rebuilt my business in the wake of the 9/11 economic downturns. I was exhausted, and I felt lost and alone. As my strength was affected, I began to doubt my abilities even more, so I saw more negative changes appearing in my body/mind.

In addition to smaller physical shifts, a new wrinkle here or there, or feeling tired, I was losing my health, and I felt that I was losing power over my own life. I sort of fell into this without realizing it was happening, until I was pretty far down the traditional path and had some huge and scary "aha" moments. How could this be happening to me? I had spent all this time studying and practicing, only to succumb to consensus aging and degeneration?

Fortunately I had prepared better than I thought. I had the background and training to meet these challenges. More importantly, I had a support group and an alternative health network that was excellent. Because my healthcare providers were mostly alternative, they did not advise extreme medicines or procedures, but took a longer view and a more natural approach. In fact, often, the worse I felt, the less they wanted to "do" to me! That was good, but I still had considerable dis-ease, and many painful symptoms.

I was shocked to realize that I had unconsciously begun to define myself by my health problems instead of defining myself as healthy. My health became measured by how well I was healing or getting better. Instead of *being* healthy and strong, I was always *getting there.* Because I was always "on my way," I was always short of the goal of health. My body was hearing and obeying this command.

Of course this contradicted everything I had studied and practiced for decades, yet it was happening to me; it felt awful. Most of us who have aging parents or relatives are familiar with the continuous stream of health complaints, detailed discussions of ailments, and doctor visits that characterize the current aging culture. I was exposed to a morphic field of aging and dis-ease so consistently over such a long time that it was affecting me dramatically.

As I worked to lift out of this downhill vortex (trying not to resist), I began writing this book. The book became a mirror for my own health and progress, and it became my teacher. As the book grew and became more complete and healthy, so did I. Writing about what I had learned allowed me to re-view, re-learn, and re-create my healthy practices. I got stronger and manifested better health, with a deeper respect for the whole range of human experience.

Importantly, this part of my journey has been fraught with "pop ups" from a sub-conscious level of deeper fears and beliefs. The closer I come to breaking through my own barriers into new existential territory, the more the frightened aspects of my being may protest. I have developed a new respect for the tactics my body/mind can use to try to protect me from something scary or distasteful.

For example, while completing this book, I began to have trouble with my eyes. They would get red, sore, and full of discharge, but there was no infection or allergy. Almost nothing would help. After much alternative therapy and work on myself, I realized that my eyes were messengers, reacting to what some deep part of me considered to be unacceptable and frightening. I used a combination of BodyTalk, EFT, meditation and the occasional prescription eye drop to get through this. The cause, however, is in my own basement of invisible, collected fears and beliefs, many of which are just not available to me at a conscious level. I continue to explore, discover, and keep going.

On our exploration of aging, we are all in for some new and possibly frightening experiences. Consensus reality on aging can be very stubborn, even among many in alternative health communities, so the renaissance voyager encounters strong challenges. Not the least of these is the feeling we all get occasionally that we are living between the old world and the new, and have no solid ground in either. In many ways, this is good, because we are living in the space of new creation. However, it can feel very lonely. Strong old programs like aging will not just disappear, but we are shifting them one person at a time, and it is incremental until it goes exponential. A new aging belief system is part of our renaissance, and we are all beginning to demonstrate new beliefs.

As Baby Boomers move ahead chronologically, we are seeing more mainstream media pieces on staying youthful, especially on women staying young into their sixties and beyond. I predict this will increase, as celebrities capitalize on demonstrating how they beat the aging game. Of course, this may have a reverse effect on the public, as we all know that famous celebrities have means that most people do not. Nevertheless, it starts an important new way of thinking about how our bodies can stay vital, attractive and healthy.

The implications of an aging renaissance are staggering. Think for a moment about a world where health prevails—where people know what that means and how to maintain and support it. Think of a world where everyone's body is considered first as healthy, strong and sovereign; where the body/mind is treated as a whole being with universal and limitless capabilities. Think of a world where the invisible is know-able and used as a resource, not feared, ridiculed, or worse, ignored.

What if instead we all joined a matrix of ascension thinking, where a renewal was supported and created? If this happened on a large enough scale, it would re-define the way we age and the whole structure, length, and quality of our lives.

What if instead of dying with money, our goal was to die with power?

14
Symbols and Other Power Tools

Man is the symbol using animal.

Kenneth Burke, "Definition of Man"

Turning then to the more emotional aspects of modern thought, we shall not be surprised to find a veritable orgy of verbomania.

C.K. Ogden and I.A. Richards,
The Meaning of Meaning

As sociologist and rhetorician Kenneth Burke points out, humans are the only animal species that creates symbols. The many and varied symbolic forms, including language, comprise what we might call a set of power tools used to manipulate or affect the consciousness of others. Even in 1923, Ogden and Richards noted the over-use of language as an emotional power tool. Symbolic manipulation never stops. It can be beneficial or harmful; it is never neutral.

Importantly, symbols can manipulate us below the level of our awareness, especially those we barely notice on a daily basis: television ads, billboards, news headlines, background music, and even lighting or various design elements we think of as decorative. To expand our awareness, we want to acknowledge the power of symbols and be aware of ways they might be used to conscript or weaken our power as well as ways they can enhance it.

Kenneth Burke and other rhetoricians have explored and described the many ways in which language and other media are used for effect as action tools. A symbolic form possesses agency, an intentional force that acts on all that perceive it.

All symbolic forms transmit energy that alters the receivers.

Marshall McLuhan, also a student of Renaissance rhetoric, was adamant about the threat of media's many forms on the hapless public: "All media works us over completely. They are so pervasive in their personal, political, economic, aesthetic, psychological, moral, ethical and social consequences that they leave no part of us untouched, unaffected, unaltered."[13]

McLuhan stands out among cultural theorists as a visionary with respect to his warnings about the use and misuse of symbolic forms. In recent years, more research has been published on the effect of symbolic forms on the energetic and physical health of humans and all life. For example, Masaro Emoto's brilliant work provides clear evidence that music, spoken and written language, and even thoughts have the power to alter the shape and nature of water molecules. Such data has obvious relevance for us as we consider the many ways in which our body/minds can be manipulated by symbols.

EVERYDAY MANIPULATORS: LANGUAGE, MUSIC, SYMBOLIC FORMS

Since language is the symbolic form we use the most to process and frame life experience, the study of language as a tool has a long history. The large body of research and scholarship we call rhetoric, which extends back to the work of Aristotle, concerns a speaker or writer's ability to use language to create an intentional effect on all levels in an audience—physical, mental, emotional, and spiritual.

The professional study of rhetoric flourished in the historical Renaissance, rekindling studies of the classical masters. Many books were devoted to guidelines for rhetoric and poetics, a study that included all language use, not just poetry. Since the clergy were the largest non-noble literate group, numerous books were printed on the rhetorical genre of the *ars praedicandi*, or art of preaching. These books taught clergy how to "install" religious beliefs and fervor in parishioners. Renaissance technology—the printing press—allowed a wider audience for language as a visual medium, so there was an acute awareness of the power of words, as well as other symbolic forms, to influence people.

Today, the many self-help resources providing verbal or written mediations or affirmation exercises also employ rhetorical arts to help facilitate outcomes using language. We use a type of self-rhetoric when we repeat affirmations, meditative mantras or when we listen to guided mediations. In these situations, we are highly aware that we are employing language as a tool to change or manipulate our perception and our experience. It is interesting that we can be very aware of the force of language in this context, but be oblivious to it later when we are being bombarded by messages on signs, on the radio, from the internet or other media. Like Ogden and Richards' "verbomania," language data is so overwhelming in the everyday world that we tend to tune it out at a conscious level, but it affects us nonetheless.

Language shows us what we believe, and what beliefs are manipulating us.

Becoming more aware of our own spoken language and the messages we hear from others around us, can provide excellent information about the sorts of belief programs we are running. For example, I often just listen to snippets of people's conversations as they pass by. Usually, they are all about some kind of problem. People tend to "rehearse" all their gripes and issues, a habit that reinforces the negatives and holds them in place.

The other day, I took notes on what I heard people talking about on their phones as they passed me. Out of twelve cell phone conversations, the results were: five interpersonal advice or gossip issues; two work-related dilemmas, which sounded like missed deadlines or incorrect work product; and five disease or personal difficulty, three of which had references like, "Well, we are getting older, you know," or "At our age we have to expect that." One guy declared, "She's never going to change and neither am I." So there! The language of these conversations provided me a pretty clear window to beliefs and perceptions we are all holding, and that are holding us from expansion into new worlds.

In my work with organizations, I have always stressed the importance of using language as a tool for creating outcomes. Even though I realize that I am biased because I have been a student and teacher of language arts, I am continually shocked at the lack of language consciousness and skill in the world of work. Perhaps more amazing is the fact that our graduate and professional-level curricula do not focus more directly on these skills, as language is our vehicle no matter what kind of work we do.

Recently, I decided to re-view books I consult and use in my leadership communication practice. The books gave me even more confirmation of the importance of language. For example, having already established that "leadership is a language game," the authors of one book go on to say that their work "treats leaders as the managers of meanings for their world. In this book, we introduce the skill of framing: a quality of communication that causes others to accept one meaning over another. It is a skill with profound consequences for behavior that influences how we and others respond to the world in which we live."[14]

Learning to use words to frame and deliver active messages, written or verbal, is obviously a crucial skill. Just think of all the money organizations spend to craft mission and vision statements or core values language. When crafted in a way that truly represents the core energy and intention of an organization, these language tools powerfully motivate and guide everyone involved with an organization. Conversely, when such value language does not represent what's really going on in the organization, it rings false to everyone (Bob's Law), and causes internal and external dissonance.

Language is fun to study, and, once we become aware of its power, we are more able to manage our incoming and outgoing messages to our benefit. This has become really a matter of survival in the modern world, where we are manipulated continuously by professionals whose sole aim is to control our behavior in some way. Marshall McLuhan prefaces his work entitled *The Mechanical Bride* with just this thought:

> "Ours is the first age in which many thousands of the best-trained individual minds have made it a full-time

> business to get inside the collective public mind. To get inside in order to manipulate, exploit, control is the object now. And to generate heat not light is the intention. To keep everybody in the helpless state engendered by prolonged mental rutting is the effect of many ads and much entertainment alike."[15]

I recommend a re-view of McLuhan's work to anyone interested in developing new ways of seeing symbolic forms, not only to detect manipulation but just for the sheer fun of seeing the many ways language and other forms can operate, whether intentional or not. For example, when creating the title for his book, *The Medium is the Massage*, McLuhan decided to change the word "Message" to "Massage," because of its connotation of manipulation, and also the play on the words "mass-age," while still calling forth the word "message," which he especially liked because the word can also be read as "mess-age."

In addition to consuming enormous amounts of language daily, reminiscent of Richards' "verbomania," we take in symbolic artifacts through many other media—visual arts, sound/music, language, and all forms of graphic symbols and patterns. All symbolic communication works through frequency as well as through learned meaning. Music affords us an easy way to think about frequency or harmonic communication, but any symbolic artifact transmits frequency, energy, or harmonics that alter the receiver.

Exercise:

The following exercise provides one way to check up on the ways that symbolic forms in your daily environment might be affecting you. This exercise is based on my *Just One Thing* model.

1. **Pick a day to keep a record of just one type of symbolic form** you encounter every day. You will be noting its effect on you: how it makes you feel, what it causes you to think about, or even what you do directly after you experience it.
2. To choose your symbolic form, **choose something you like to notice.** Maybe you enjoy music, or you like art, design elements, shapes and colors, or like me, you love language. If you do choose language, you may also want to

narrow your focus further to a specific type of language use, such as emails or one medium, like the newspaper or music lyrics.

3. **Record your findings**, using whatever method is easiest for you. You may want to jot notes on a small pad periodically, or use a voice recorder. Note particularly when you find that the form is affecting you strongly, and note how it makes you feel or think differently.
4. **Check in on your progress** a couple of times during the day. Maybe you have discovered enough before the day is done! If so, then you are ready for the next step.
5. At the end of your day, or when you are finished, **reflect on the way you have experienced the power of that particular symbolic form.** Debrief yourself on how best to release negative messages you may have ingested and protect yourself from future ones. If you had really great positive experiences, decide how to make sure you take in more of them.
6. Feel free to **do this exercise anytime**—after you do it once or twice, you will find you become generally more alert to symbolic forms and their power.

This type of exercise can also be done with a partner. The partner can help you by using applied kinesiology (AK) or muscle testing to determine if a particular symbolic form strengthens or weakens you.[16]

The results of AK testing for the effect of everyday symbolic forms can be dramatic. For example, just looking at the front page of almost any newspaper will weaken most people. This happens because, as Masaru Emoto proved in his experiments with water, the body is negatively affected by painful or harmful messages in any format. The typically negative content of a front page—in pictures and language—transmits a multi-layered negative frequency which will cause a body/mind to weaken. A negative, or weak AK test may also occur in response to many types of popular music, and to many TV or other media programs.

One day I decided to listen closely to the lyrics of popular songs on the radio. You will not be surprised that many of the messages I heard were violent, negative, or somehow unhealthy. Traditionally, what we call romantic songs are often sad, laments for the loss or death of a loved one. Sadness seems tame compared to the frequency of many popular songs transmitting messages of physical violence or sexual aggression; music and lyrics often combine to transmit a very rough, unsettling effect. The experience feels almost like the Renaissance verbal terrors set to pop music. Just listen for a couple of hours. It is easy to forget that our body/mind takes all this in and processes it, even if we are not paying attention. At some level, we hear this and it affects us deeply.

Sometimes I get a song stuck in my head and it won't go away. I learned recently that this is called an "earworm," a creepy but perfect metaphor for the sinister way this works in one's brain. All day long, the words and melody keep looping through my mind. I know this happens to lots of folks, and it is a common programming goal of advertising jingles.

Branding is all about the instant association of a product with a symbol. I can still sing many of the advertising ditties from the 1950s. Examples include, "You'll wonder where the yellow went, when you brush your teeth with Pepsodent," or the Maxwell House coffee song, which used only a rhythmic sequence of musical notes to mimic the sounds of a coffee percolator. Whenever I become aware that some language or music is affecting me, I pay attention. Why does it come up when it does? Why does it persist? Why does it leave?

Recently, while revising the section of the book on the invisible power of emotions, I found myself singing a refrain from the 1960s song called "Chains," which was most famously recorded by The Beatles. The lyrics that repeated in my mind were the first three lines: "Chains, my baby's got me locked up in chains/And they ain't the kind that you can see/Whoa, oh, these chains of love got a hold on me, yeah."[17] That song lasted for days, but I had pulled it up from my subconscious, where it had been living and active for fifty years! I did not connect the song to my own experience, until I took time to think about what was going on when it came up.

I encourage all readers to explore the effects of symbolic power tools. Just understanding that these symbolic forms are used as active tools increases a person's power. Learning to manage the affects of symbolic manipulation can create a life-altering shift toward health and power.

Freedom begins with awareness.

Sex: Everyone's Favorite Saboteur

Everything in the world is about sex except sex. Sex is about power.

Oscar Wilde

Sex is a primary power area – it is our life-giving vehicle. Our sex drive motivates us to procreate because of its commanding force and allure. Sexuality provides energy, entertainment, mystery, and it's fun. In short, sex is powerful and it is about power on many levels. Because of this, sex can manipulate and sabotage us as well as please us. Especially now, when stress is high and we need a feel-good escape, sex may have even more appeal than usual. For all these reasons, it pays to re-view this crucial power area. The more we understand about our powerful sexual resources, the better we can use them for our enjoyment and the more easily we can avoid situations targeting sexuality to manipulate us.

Understanding the invisible aspects of our sexuality reveals new worlds of both vulnerability and power.

Sexuality certainly demonstrates the 99% invisible rule. Our sexual instincts and power rely upon a complex system of invisible drivers. Sexual manipulation triggers ancient, deep core programs for survival of our species, targeting many of the most crucial drivers – all of our senses, emotions, memories and thoughts above and below the level of our awareness.

All our powerful sexual triggers can also be used to influence our behavior and beliefs. We are bombarded daily by sensory data using sexual content to drive consumer spending, and influence our decision-making about almost everything. Even though we may be aware of being manipulated, we still do not educate ourselves adequately about the red-hot nature of this "iceberg"!

In addition to the overt sexual content we may almost not notice anymore, entertainment media are using more and more archetypal sexual content. Mythical demons, warriors, dragons, and various underworld creatures populate our television and theater screens. I don't know about you, but most of these heroes, heroines, and demons seem a lot sexier to me than they ever did in books, or even in my imagination.

Current media also target the darker, edgier qualities of our sexuality. A look at a few magazine covers will demonstrate this. Although most self-help or wellness magazines feature bright, clean (but still sexy) men or women on their covers, fashion, entertainment, and many other publications depict darker or even taboo scenes. One sees more "girl on girl" or *ménage a trois* images in fashion images, for example, and trends toward vampire-like makeup or darkly dramatic eyes, blood red lips and nails, and so on. The clean look remains, but why not trigger the darker primal side for some extra profit?

We know that erotic movies, literature, and other media stimulate our sexuality by stimulating our thoughts, which trigger emotional and physical responses. But even though we may realize what is happening, the tactics still work. Advertising makes use of these triggers effectively to sell everything, from soap to songs and beyond. The media floods us with sexual and sensual images—the hotter the better. One even wonders if we have become desensitized from all this advertising stimulation to the point where we need the extra stimulation of the taboos to ignite the triggers.

The average person is the pawn, not the profiteer in our commercial sex culture.

The invisible power resources of our sexuality importantly include the enormous creative life-force energy known as kundalini. "Kundalini" is a Sanskrit word often translated as "coiled energy" and has come to be represented as a coiled snake sitting at the base of the human spine. One author defines the word as "the life force of the body that when fully actualized, leads to living life as an enlightened sage."[18] The coiled energy of kundalini has extreme explosive and creative power, which untrained people may feel during orgasm or possibly at other times. When awakened, kundalini will travel up the spine channel, awakening chakra energy centers as it goes.

Developing and learning to control kundalini has been the life work of many masters and students in a variety of disciplines, including the yogic study of tantra. Probably, most people think of tantra as a sexual practice, which it is, but not exclusively, as it is first and foremost a development and discipline of human power. Practitioners are taught by masters to take this energy and its use very seriously. Misuse or untrained awakening of kundalini can even cause death.

Aside from yogis and people in the alternative community, I do not know many people who have been informed about the existence, much less the use or control of their kundalini. Somehow, though, confirming Bob's Law again, everyone knows that their sexuality is a powerful force, no matter how they experience it. When I first moved to South Beach— infamous as a place where people come to have lots of sex— I was amazed at some of the behaviors I observed. It seemed to me that a sort of sexual morphic field was in place here, and people came to jump into it, like diving into the ocean.

The South Beach energy field seems to switch on people's sex generators, including of course the kundalini energy. A friend in Chicago explained it to me like this, "You see, Doc, the folks come down there, and, between the sun, the energy field, and the ocean (not to mention anything else) their kundalini gets all stirred up. Not knowing what it is or what else to do with those sensations, they just have lots of sex, exhaust themselves, and call it a vacation!" Becoming more aware of the power of a place to stimulate our sexual energy might provide a better and safer vacation.

Minding or managing the kundalini is just one part of practicing what we might call "energetic (or invisible) safe sex." Another would be an expanded awareness of the profound energetic exchange that occurs in a sexual encounter. For our purposes, understanding the enormous invisible power of our sexuality affords us a new way to view a sexual encounter as an intimate energy exchange—a comingling of emotional, mental, physical, and spiritual energy and frequency.

Safe sex is an energy issue.

With this view of sex as consciousness and frequency-based, we can re-view the definition of safe sex. Most people would probably say they practice safe sex by protecting themselves physically from sexually transmitted diseases through the use of condoms. But what about the energetic, mental, and emotional threats of sex? I think that even in consensual sex, a lot of real damage often occurs at the invisible body levels – the emotional, mental bodies and the energy field itself. In addition to causing emotional hurt or other undesirable invisible body results, emotional or energetic pathogens may weaken the physical body's ability to resist microbial threats.

Because sex is a power exchange, there are power dynamics involved, but the most critical may be the ones we do not usually consider. The fun of a one-night stand can be easily ruined after the fact by its emotional and energetic "payback." Why else would popular culture use terms like "hit and run" to describe this type of encounter?[19] This is Bob's Law at work again, but it is easy to forget.

Even more importantly, the intimate connections of a sexual encounter co-mingle both partners' entire energy and consciousness. The term for this in quantum physics is "entanglement." Although the word has negative connotations for most people, in the scientific sense it is value neutral, but indicates a powerful force. The more intimately we engage with another person or being, the more deeply all facets of us are joined, and this connection becomes a permanent part of us. We actually receive and retain data from all facets of our partner's life and all of his or her past and present relationships. This immense concept should not stop us from having fun, but it certainly provides us another good reason to be careful.

Increased awareness of invisible resources and of the impact of negative or harmful energy can help anyone make better decisions regarding sexual partners. Also, we might not be having anywhere near the great sex we could have if we learned more about how to use this powerful asset.

Exercise: Investigating Your Sexual Programs

Because we all consume tons of sexual content that may not be registering at the level of everyday awareness, once in a while it pays to do a little investigation. The purpose is to dig for programming that affects or manipulates our sexuality. Here are some of the questions I use.

1. When I think of a sexy man (or woman) I think of _______________ (name) because ___________________.
2. I think of myself as sexy and having sexual power (yes/no).
3. Sex is important to me (yes/no).
4. I feel sexy when I __________________________________.
5. The three most important influences on my sexual image of myself have been__________________________________.
6. In my current (or most recent) sexual relationship, I feel that levels of intimacy, energy, and power were healthy (yes/no) because __________________________________.
7. Three products or services I may have purchased because of sexually motivated advertising are ______________________________.

You can make up your own questions and do more investigation. The exercise helps you to decide if there are ways you can better "command the force" of your sexual power, then make changes. Answers to your questions may change as you change, so you can discover new aspects of yourself each time.

Sexuality involves all of our body/mind interfaces, functioning at all levels—above and below our awareness. Once we begin to discover more about this crucial resource, we can start to explore and reclaim our own sexual identity and power. There may be a new world there too!

TV: STILL #1 PROGRAMMER

To put it briefly, man cannot trust himself when using his own artefacts.

Marshall McLuhan, *Laws of Media*

Although smart phones, tablets, and laptops certainly expose us to continuous media and frequency manipulation, television probably still represents our most widespread programming vehicle. In McLuhan's words, TV is an "artefact" that has become embedded in our daily lives and affects all aspects of our being. It is ironic that we call television shows "programs," because that is exactly how they function: they perpetuate and manipulate a variety of invisible programs that affect us at all levels. There are certainly positive aspects to TV shows, but it pays to be aware of the challenges the medium presents.

Television works on us at all levels.

TV uses an increasingly large (huge flat screen) and life-like (HD) audio-visual medium to trigger and manipulate all our mental and emotional components. In addition, the television itself emits electromagnetic frequency which can alter or harm us.

Jerry Mander's 1978 book, *Four Arguments for the Elimination of Television,* sums up the issues pretty well. Commenting on the book's arguments, the author summarizes the threat:

> Television has effects, very important effects, aside from content. They organize society in a certain way. They give power to a very small number of people to speak into the brains of everyone else in the system night after night after night with images that make people turn out in a certain kind of way. It affects the psychology of the people who watch. It increases the passivity of people who watch. It changes family relationships. It changes understandings of nature. It flattens perception....[20]

Mander's work did not address content, just the effect of the medium itself. But a brief re-view of how the typical nightly content might affect us provides a way to become aware of the manipulative possibilities. If I turn the TV on any major network station starting at 5:00 p.m., I get a lineup something like this:

- 5:00-6:30: **News** programs, which are mostly bad news—stories and images of murder, theft and unrest in the world; wars, violence, economic instability, and the list goes on. The message is that the world is a dangerous and potentially lethal place. There is always at least one interview with a crying, emotionally damaged person and at least one picture of an accident or bodies being carted to a hospital, or both. This emotional/mental assault repeats itself in an endless loop. Lately, I notice that the news shows try to put on some positive content, but often it is a "Good Samaritan" story involving abused animals, the family of murder victims, or some other semi-tragic situation, which still targets key emotional triggers.

- 6:30-8:00: **"Celebrity News" shows** – various programs that feed the viewer the "inside" stories of all the media stars we are encouraged to focus on instead of paying attention to our own lives, families, and creations. This type of celebrity content has a double-edged effect. On the one hand, it separates viewers from the celebrities. Viewers are lesser beings, regular people who can only sit by and watch all these giant celebrities. On the other hand, it provides viewers a sense of false power, by implying that we have some access to some special information. Further, our cultural "idols" are usually doing bad things— being arrested for some form of violent behavior, alcohol or drug use. Night after night they model negative behavior. The message sent to viewers seems to be: "This behavior is what makes you a star."
- 8:00-10:00 or 11:00: **Prime Time**, which includes:
    - **"Reality" shows** in which people are filmed in what is supposedly a "real" situation, to compete for something by participating in a variety of stressful activities with lots of emotional display. Reality shows really work over the viewers' emotional bodies, while blurring the fiction/reality line further every year. I watch some of these, by the way, and like them, but I always want to make sure I stay awake to what is happening.

      Reality shows devoted to competition in all areas of performance, sport or interpersonal behavior, are a growing part of prime time entertainment. When I watch, my emotional message system is all lit up. I identify with the contestants, of course—they are real people! That could be me. The bad news is that the shows can easily manipulate my emotions to the degree that I relate personally to them. The good news is that the performers are real people, and the market wants that—to see regular human beings become "famous" and powerful. So in a way, these shows can be seen as a harbinger of the human renaissance – a nightly display of human strength and ability, and of the many talents we possess.

- **"Drama" shows** that are all about crime, usually including but not limited to murder, often related to abusive sexual activity, and, of course, lots and lots of violence. The proliferation of criminal investigation shows boggles the mind. The increasingly graphic content takes a toll on viewers, many of whom may be children or adolescents, and has a numbing effect on the emotional system. I once changed the channel in prime time five times in a few minutes, only to find dead bloody bodies on every station—either on autopsy tables (why has this captured our attention?) or in some death scene.

  Perhaps as an indicator of the growing interest in the invisible aspects of life, many popular shows feature either supernatural beings or people with "extra-sensory" powers. Unfortunately, many of these characters are not positively portrayed. The characters with expanded sensory or mental capabilities are often misfits. The supernatural beings are often evil – witches, human hybrids, vampires, werewolves and so on. These stories tend to access our "darker" archetypal databases for maximum effect—and ratings. Interestingly, though, the supernatural subject matter indicates that there is awareness of a renaissance trend to discover and use the "invisible world." Popular culture does a good job mirroring our interests since we are the market.

- 10:00-11:00: Time for the **NEWS again!**

Advertisements as Programming Devices

TV programs are frequently interrupted by advertisements, many chanting negative messages that weaken or manipulate us. Everyone laughs about the burgeoning number of ads for prescription drugs, which have some ultra-fast voice droning the "side effects include" information. Of course, you must "ask your doctor" everything, including "if you are healthy enough for sexual activity." To make matters worse, what if these are just the messages we can detect? Subliminal messaging has been used for decades. This comprises an invisible frontier on its own. Even if we say we pay no attention to these messages, we are taking them into our being, and they do affect us.

The advertisements during the day target a different market than the ones at night, but use the same tactics. During the day, ads seem to trigger different survival fears: accidents, disabilities, legal and criminal issues. These ads mingle with pitches for various technical degree programs to help viewers re-start their lives. The messages assume a desperation and lack of power in the audience, and by rehearsing the issues, they support the problems. This type of "programming" damages our power base, triggering our minds, emotions, and bodies to operate in ways that are not optimal, while promising to improve our lives.

To do your own detection exercise with TV, just turn it on anytime and prepare to be amazed at what you see and experience. You can record the various messages or images that you find and how they affect you. You don't have to watch for long – less than an hour should give you reams of data.

Like social media, television has begun to reflect mass culture's growing interest in real human beings.

In addition to focusing on real people or aspects of their lives, TV also increasing presents programs about extra-ordinary or paranormal people. Some of these portrayals are negative, depicting extra-ordinary humans who are misfits or evil-doers. The evil supernatural characters include witches, vampires, demons, and the like, which are prevalent and becoming almost like caricatures. However, other shows depict intuitives, psychics, or others who use what I might call "whole brain" power in a positive way in life and work, although they may be misfits or children. On balance, though, this trend signals a growing renaissance awareness.

If we commit to creating healthier home environments, our use of TV will change drastically. In order to provide healthier entertainment, TV programming would likewise have to change. Any content which abuses or intends to manipulate people would have to be deleted and replaced with content that was helpful or actually just entertaining. Current models for this do exist: public television is the best example. If television is only supported by consumer-targeted advertising, can it ever be optimal? Can we change the way we believe and act in the marketplace to drive consumer economics in a more healthy direction? I think the answer is yes, but not unless we realize the power that we give up to TV by submitting to its content, manipulation, and even its electromagnetic frequency (EMF) disturbance.

Courses on the nature and function of TV and other media could be taught in schools starting very early, and could be made available at low or no cost as continuing education to the general public. Courses could include information on ways to test for harmful content and unhealthy EMFs (from TV as well as other devices). Courses could also articulate the potential hazards of violent, sexually-based, or fear-based content and provide people with ways to balance the effects. Everyone actually knows at some level that we need to do something about the threats of harmful media.

As always, it is we, the consumers, who will drive change. A new world deserves a new way to use our most powerful media.

Part Four

The New World of Your Power

Introduction

We are all on a Hero's journey. We have all experienced a Call to Adventure. You don't have to be a Hercules or Achilles, or Perseus or Odysseus to be a hero. Consider the power you exercise right here, right now.

Jean Houston, *The Wizard of Us*

We are closer than we may think to a full-out renaissance. I hope this book has made clear that we have access to immense power within and around us that we can use every day, in any situation. We can see the Human Renaissance as our "Call to Adventure," an adventure that continues throughout a rich, creative, healthy life.

Throughout the book, we have discussed many principles and techniques to help us discover new aspects of ourselves, our world, and our power as human beings. We have reviewed the immense body of literature and wisdom that supports our exploration and provides data to confirm the validity of our endeavor. We have considered various features of our invisible resources, ways to use them, and challenges they may present.

This final chapter reviews important individual keys to this exciting new way of living. After reading an early version of this book, a friend asked the ultimate question, "If we have all the great information and research and work, why aren't more people using this knowledge in everyday life?" Here I describe key activities and techniques I have found most helpful to realizing a renaissance in real life.

15
Keys to the New World

Key #1: Identify Belief Barricades

As we have seen from the beginning of the book, beliefs and belief systems act as powerful unseen masters. Beliefs determine much of what we think, see, and do. Our beliefs can block our vision or convince us not to explore. Let's look at some of the possible belief barricades that could be addressed to make your journey easier and more productive.

One important barricade is the belief that exploration, discovery, and adventures are for heroic figures, not for you or me. We are taught that all significant explorations are Epic endeavors, which cannot be done by regular people, and certainly not in everyday life. Jean Houston asks us to set this belief aside, to realize that we all possess heroic power and we are each heroes on our own adventure. Renaissance Man and thought pioneer Joseph Campbell worked for years to teach people the many human faces of the hero, and ways that the hero's journey was really a journey we all take.[1] Nevertheless, the words "hero" or "magic" or "adventure" can trigger limiting beliefs.

Another aspect of this block is our belief that any type of exploration or discovery is a huge undertaking, like Admiral Byrd's polar explorations, or climbing Mount Everest. That's one reason we believe these activities are reserved for special people with special knowledge, skills, and personalities. Thinking about actually using some of the material in this book, for example might cause a reaction like, "This is such a huge endeavor, I would have to spend years of study to learn so many different topics and genres. I am no physicist, philosopher or doctor!"

We can easily forgive ourselves for believing that we may lack the expertise or time required for this type of self-discovery. We may find ourselves overwhelmed by the prospect of learning even a piece of the immense body of New Age material, which represents a daunting combination of philosophical, spiritual, psychological, medical, mystical, and advanced scientific information. I hope this book has shown, however, that such information is accessible and we can sort through it to determine the key principles. We need not be intimidated by the multiple perspectives, languages, or labels used to describe our innate resources. Your body/mind functions without labels. Further, you already know much of this; remember Bob's Law.

We also may be held back by cultural beliefs about material we label as New Age, which to some means it 1) is not applicable in the Real World and 2) is inappropriate in the world of work, in corporate or organizational cultures. I asked a friend who is recently retired from an executive position and has thirty years of corporate experience, why she thought so few people in the workplace take advantage of this wisdom. She replied that business was all about the "bottom line," not just profits, but the process of getting there through analysis of "hard data," and "real outcomes." I was struck by the beliefs that her comments revealed about what constituted "data" or "real outcomes."

My friend's words also helped me remember how it felt to me to be both an alternative and traditional person working in the traditional corporate belief matrix. When I felt discomfort, it was based on my own belief that I must always choose to be either this OR that. When I was working inside a corporate culture, was I choosing to be that (corporate) me, or could I still be this (corporate, academic, alternative) me? Of course, I embody and use all of these aspects of myself. I had to embrace my own diversity. Most people are similarly multi-faceted, so the pressure to fit into any one cultural mold seems counter to just being human. Yet, it is a challenge we face daily.

The 99% invisible rule is operating whether we choose to ignore or embrace it.

Finally, a classic belief barricade to any form of self-development is "I don't have enough ___ (fill in the blank: money, time, energy, or other)." This block also relies on our basic belief in human limitation. If your belief block is cost-related, remember that changing your mind is free. If you perceive a time block, you can use the time envelope technique to give you some room. This book provides a number of techniques, exercises, and resources to help move those barricades.

If we can recognize our belief barricades and clear them to allow new perspectives, we open countless doors to fresh ideas and outcomes. I am sure this list of beliefs and belief areas is just a start. You can discover your own. The exercise itself frees us by opening our perception.

Key #2: Don't Let Fear of Change Stop You

Belief barricades are powered by fear. Fear of change is an automatic response for most people. We fear change because we fear the unknown. Changing any aspect of our lives can bring up all our core fears about loss of control, safety and security.

As we grow and evolve, we also challenge all aspects of our previously secure identity. This causes understandable doubt and fear. Once we can locate our own areas of fear, we can take control by remembering the polarity principle. We ease out of fear not by resisting it, but by acknowledging it and moving forward with enhanced awareness and compassion for ourselves. Chapter 10 of this book dealt specifically with fear as a saboteur; here we revisit this important key area by looking at some new approaches to use as tools.

The beliefs we have already reviewed demonstrate some of our fears about losing control, power, ability, time, or money. These may be excuses to avoid the huge fear of radical change. We somehow believe it is possible to change *too much* and if we do, we 1) instantly become some other person, so 2) we no longer fit into our old life and 3) everyone around us notices this and reacts negatively toward us. I'd like to address briefly each of these three fears about change to provide a starting place for new thought.

Fear is normal. We have to do our best to move through it if we want to experience a more expansive life.

First, change is seldom instant; it usually begins as incremental. I teach and use the "Just One Thing" approach to change (see Chapter 8), and it works nicely. Very few people have total enlightenment experiences and walk out of their house the next day completely different. For most people, just taking the first steps to any change makes all the next steps easier. The result is an organic change that can go exponential at any time!

Second, as we shift our ways of thinking, seeing, and being, we do experience dissonance with our old life, but that does not mean our new perspectives are incorrect. As I have described in my personal stories, living in what seemed to be two worlds for many years caused me more than a few sleepless nights and anxious moments. Now, however, there is good news for explorers. The renaissance is already taking place. Although not fully mainstream, the worlds are already combining, so the duality you will experience is much less than it was in the 1980s or even ten years ago. A growing field of alternative consciousness has prepared the way for anyone who wants to discover new aspects of themselves and our world. That provides huge relief, and faster outcomes.

Finally, we can accept our tendencies to judge, and the fear that can create. As we encounter our judgments, we can use them as learning tools, opportunities to shift situations. When I worry about negative criticism from others, I try to remember that I am first judging myself. I actually have no idea how others will respond to whatever I am doing, I make it all up before they ever get a chance. So that means that if I can better control my own negative, fearful judgments, I will most likely not attract similar judgments from others. I often do this by first locating what it is I fear, then trying to re-write the story with positive, accepting outcomes. This exercise gives me confidence to move forward. Once I do, I find people are usually very accepting and even helpful.

On the other hand, there is a mainstream tendency to judge and censure new ideas and innovations, as we have seen in many gruesome tales from history. Chapter 2 reviewed some of the terrible fates of Renaissance authors and scientists, for example. While we may not be able to eradicate this human tendency to push back to the perceived threat of innovation, we can start to understand it better. We can also try to control our own fears about new or different ideas, especially when they dramatically challenge concepts we have used to define ourselves and to feel powerful and safe.

Scientist and author Gerald Pollack summarizes the difficulties he faced when confronting the *status quo* scientific community with new ideas about the principles of water. His words could well apply to principles of our human renaissance. He asks, "If these principles are as useful as claimed, then why have they remained secret for so long? How have they escaped inclusion in the repository of common understanding?"[2]

Pollack then provides four possible reasons for this challenge, three of which apply perfectly to our renaissance challenges. I present them below with my own added emphasis in bold:

1. "**few people can conceive that the basics can remain open to question** … today's science rewards those who focus narrowly on trendy areas, leaving little room for questioning widely taught foundational science … the incentive to question fundamentals has all but vanished" (339).
2. "**intellectual timidity.** Relying on received wisdom feels safer than dealing with the uncertainties of revolutionary disruption" (339).
3. "**outright fear** … questioning the prevailing wisdom has always been a risky business, in science as elsewhere" (339-40).

Pollack concludes, "These obstacles have combined to produce a long-term stall" in discoveries about water. I believe the same type of "long-term stall" has been experienced as we have waited for acceptance or use of alternative thought and methods to enter our lives. Now it is time, as Pollack suggests to "crank up the engine."[3] Our engine is the human renaissance.

KEY #3: DEVELOP AND USE A RENAISSANCE TOOLKIT

A crucial key to our renaissance experience is to make use of tools and techniques that help facilitate enhanced awareness and new, more positive outcomes in real life. Many chapters in the book contain exercises and references that provide such tools. In addition to those, I will suggest a few more in the section below. I also offer you access to many more tools on the Human Renaissance website: www.humanrenaissance.com Please remember this is not medical or professional health advice, but a description of what has worked for me.

FOUNDATION TOOLS

Harness the Power of Your Mind

Establishing a strong mental foundation for development is critical, especially because we are working in the 99% invisible realms. Some form of meditation is crucial to accessing and learning about our invisible power tools. Meditation techniques are ancient human power tools. Many people now meditate regularly, creating a strong matrix. Every time we meditate, we join this matrix and tap into its advanced power. Thus, the techniques are easier and faster to learn, and the results are more powerful.

It is very easy to find books, recordings, and DVDs to learn a meditation technique.[4] I now use a combination of transcendental meditation (TM) and Buddhist sitting meditation where I allow myself to be present with whatever comes up, acting as observer of my own states, ideas, fears, desires, and so on. In addition, I use recorded creative visualization meditations, and I also create my own. The point for me is to remember to sit with myself as often as possible, to experience the discipline, and the comfort of the discipline.

Once you are meditating daily, you can change and grow your own practice. The key is to establish a regular practice and just try to stick to it. When you miss a morning meditation, take time at lunch or after dinner, or even just before you go to sleep. You can fit a little bit in. You can use the Time Envelope Tool! I also highly recommend using your meditation to create a mental place, a "palace of possibilities," or "workshop" where you can go to heal, rest, and create.

Part of training your internal resources is reminding yourself to remain open and aware, especially when things get difficult and you are tempted to fall back on old habits. I find that I often need to remind myself that I HAVE internal resources – I can take a moment out of the fray of everyday life for a quick mental break, or to check in with myself. It helps to re-view my tools during the day. I can ask questions like the following: What am I resisting? Do I need to reverse polarity? Am I aware of what life is showing me as a learning video? Am I being influenced by a belief or manipulated by language, symbols or fear? What messages are coming to me that I may not be fully hearing, seeing, or feeling?

Record Your Discoveries

Keeping a record of your discoveries, questions, and progress really pays off. Because I still like to write by hand, I use a spiral-bound lined journal, and I have fun getting different types of journals that fit my current mood or phase. You can do this any way you want: voice recordings, videos, or writing on your tablet or PC. Try to record things shortly after you experience them, especially when you are actively engaged in any exploration. This allows you to go back and see what you did; if you are like me, you may forget interesting details.

Tip: When journaling, I write only on the right side of the page, so when I re-view, I can make notes on the left side. The journal acts as a rich resource for me later. My journals helped me a lot with this book.

Move!

Our bodies and our energies are constantly in motion and we need movement to stay healthy. This sounds trite, but it is easy to forget, and movement has many aspects. To be effective, movement need not be difficult, and it does not have to be what we think of as "working out," although that is certainly good. Energy exercises like Tai Chi, Chi Gong, or many forms of Yoga, are pleasant, low stress ways to move the body's energy and connect to the energy around us. This type of exercise is critical. I use a combination of energy exercises and yoga stretches each morning to get ready for my day.

Beyond that, any way you can add movement and a bit of strength training is great. Not everyone can join a health club or hire a trainer, but almost everyone can stretch, walk, or move in some way every day. For the last thirty years, I have walked or jogged for at least thirty minutes several times a week. I use various toning DVDs at home, and occasionally take classes or have a session with a trainer. I do most of my movement on my own, at little or no cost. I also make it a point to study and learn about how to move and strengthen my body.

Over the years I have found that any time I have made a significant evolutionary shift in my life, I have simultaneously strengthened my body. I believe the old phrase, "healthy body, healthy mind" is right. It's easier to feel confident when the body is open and alive and strong. Finally, I try to remember to listen to my body's needs; they are often different from what I believed I "should" do, or what someone else has prescribed.

Create New Habits

Of course, all this activity is easier when it becomes a routine positive habit. Like any other new behavior, creating habits focused on your renaissance development requires that you initially set aside a regular time to practice, and commit to doing so. Otherwise, you can be back to the old routine in no time. I like the early morning for journaling, meditating, or doing basic energy exercises. This takes me only about an hour (often less), and I am ready to go. In the evening, I like to walk, run, or do strength training before dinner.

I always try to remember that "it's incremental until it goes exponential!" The process may seem cumbersome at first, but it will become a habit, and then it can surprise you with results beyond what you might imagine. If you are having trouble staying in a routine, consider having a good friend or a partner act as your coach for a few weeks, just checking in on you to see how you are getting along. You may also want to put reminders on your PC and/or your phone, something that reminds you that it's time to focus on you.

I provide many renaissance tools on my website at www.humanrenaissance.com. I invite you to visit, take advantage of the resources, and contact me to learn more.

Key # 4: Never Stop Exploring, Learning, and Evolving

For me, this is the most important key. Exploration, discovery, and continuous evolution become habits of mind, ways of living that keep us young, healthy and vibrant. If we can remain open, curious, and excited to discover new things each day, we enhance all aspects of our lives and the lives of those around us. The human renaissance starts with you, but it extends to everyone.

Individually, we can each do our best to learn and explore our own abilities in spite of conflicting messages from our upbringing, education or culture. Our enhanced awareness can be our best navigation tool, and, as we have discussed, we can learn and employ effective techniques to keep us healthy and to help us make good choices. We can pass our expanded self-awareness and worldview to our children, grandchildren and anyone we teach or mentor. Our models can help them to be optimal powerful people, with a continuing curiosity, openness, and joy in discovery.

Collectively, we can work together to actively apply renaissance principles within traditional structures, in organizations, schools and universities. We can design educational programs and curricula that teach about our innate abilities, and how to use them to create health and other positive outcomes. We have the knowledge, the human resources, and the technology platforms available to bring knowledge and change to millions of people. We can (re)connect ourselves, and, in so doing, as Jules Michelet put it (see Chapter 1), we "re-find" ourselves as whole, powerful human beings.

Bob's Law works: people already know about this renaissance.

In conclusion, a new focus on developing ourselves as human beings can act as our renaissance engine, allowing us to be healthier and more powerful. The discovery of our invisible assets, and our commitment to using them for everyone's benefit, will be the keys to a new world. Once we begin to know who we are, we can also realize that we are not only equal—we are one. What happens to anyone of us affects us all—and we have the opportunity and the challenge now to use that huge collective force to create miracles.

We have an enormous task, but we also have enormous resources. We can refocus our human, technological, curricular, and financial resources and collaborate more fully to create a large-scale shift.

This book never ends. It is carried on in your thoughts, intentions, and actions as we all move forward to explore and create the future. Thank you for sharing the journey of this book. I look forward to working with you as we realize our exciting human renaissance.

Acknowledgements

This book would not exist without the love and support of many friends, family members, colleagues, healers, and teachers. I am deeply grateful to everyone who has helped me along the way. If I do not mention your name here, please know that you are included in my intention.

To my family, living and already passed, I thank you for being there unconditionally throughout my journey, as only a family can be. To my long-time friends, I send much gratitude for also being family and for cheering me on. Special thanks to Alex Garza, Nancy Krauss, Karen Aronowitz, Thomas Pecora, Todd Nordstrom, Steven Holden-Style, Jerry Laurain, Paula Sperduto, Peter Cazalet, Walter Chao, and Terri Dodge. Great love and gratitude to my BodyTalk family members, especially Janet Parker, Janet Galipo, Susan Schiedel, Cecilia Shaw, and my "sister," Patricia McManus. Endless gratitutde to Boodles, my cat companion, for her powerful teaching and healing, all the fun, and those amazing naps.

Many thanks to Janet Galipo for discovering my much-delayed book in a BodyTalk session, and helping me to move things along. Gratitude to Ian Forrester for keeping my computers going. Extra thanks to those who read this book in its early forms and gave such helpful feedback and suggestions: Steven Holden-Style, Nancy Krauss, Alex Garza, Jo Manning, and huge thanks to Patricia McManus, who should be a professional editor!

I thank the many healthcare professionals without whom I could not have learned and experienced so much about my innate resources; without them I might not be here at all. Deep gratitude to Jerry Roese, who started me on my renaissance path and for whom there is no proper thanks. Thanks to Ieva Wright, Andrea Rentea, Kathleen Aharoni, and Don Pelegrini, who kept me going during many developmental years in Chicago. In Florida, to Kirby Hotchner, Walter Chao, and Dot Larkin and repeat thanks to my BodyTalk family and Terri Dodge.

Special thanks to Donna Eden, whose exuberance and commitment to teaching people about innate health and power continue to inspire me and so many others. Thanks to John Veltheim, for founding, teaching, and continuing to evolve the remarkable BodyTalk system. Gratitude to all authors whose works appear in my text, notes, and bibliography for being my teachers whenever I needed you, day or night, over many years. I am indebted to each of you for the learning and the confirmation that the human renaissance was actually happening.

Thanks also to the many clients and organizational leaders who have trusted me with the crucial and often delicate task of organizational and professional development. Special gratitude to Bob MacAyeal, former colleague, friend, and organizational development (OD) mentor who taught me to trust my OD intuition, and is the author of "Bob's Law," which continues to guide me through my career and life.

Finally, deep gratitude to Creator God and to all my fellow human beings who carry such divinity and power and live so bravely every day in this challenging world.

Notes

Part One: Our Renaissance

1. Jules Michelet was the first historian to use the term "renaissance" to describe the reawakening of art, science, philosophy, and culture that took place in Europe in the fifteenth through seventeenth centuries. Michelet wrote a multi-volume history of France. The epigraph is from the volume in which the term first appears, *Histoire De France Au Seizieme Siecle: Renaissance* (Paris: Chamerot, Librarie-Editeur, 1855), Kindle edition, location 47 of 4124. The original reads: "...va de Colomb a Copernic, de Copernic a Galilee, de la decouverte de la terre a oelle du ciel. L'homme s'y est retrouve lui-meme."
2. Robert O. Becker and Gary Selden, *The Body Electric: Electromagnetism and the Foundation of Life* (NY: William Morrow, 1985), p. 70. I highly recommend this book, not only for its wealth of information on science, health, and tissue regeneration, but also for its clear and humorous descriptions of the challenges innovators face.
3. Although there are many works dealing with the life and career of Elizabeth I, I suggest Alison Weir's insightful biography *The Life of Elizabeth I* (NY: Ballantine Books, 2008). For an interesting look at her leadership genius, see Alan Axelrod's *Elizabeth I CEO: Strategic Lessons from the Leader Who Built an Empire* (NY: Prentice Hall Books, 2000).
4. This phrase was first used by Walt Kelly, creator of the cartoon character Pogo, in his foreword to *The Pogo Papers* (1952-3), then later on a poster for Earth Day in 1970. For this information and to see Pogo and the poster, go to http://igopogo.com/we_have_met.htm/.

5. Many thanks to Bob MacAyeal.
6. The sci-fi series *Doctor Who* is a BBC production that began in 1963 and ran until 1989. It was brought back in 2005, and celebrated a fifty-year anniversary in 2013. The BBC has called *Doctor Who* "the longest running science fiction series of all known time" on its site: http://bbcamericashop.com/. You can explore *Doctor Who* on the official BBC site, http://bbc.co.uk/programmes/, and rent or purchase the many episodes.
7. See William Ury, *Getting Past No: Negotiating Your Way from Confrontation to Cooperation* (NY: Bantam Books, 1993), p. 78. For the classic study of framing as the way we organize our life experience, see Erving Goffman's *Frame Analysis: An Essay on the Organization of Experience* (Boston: Northeastern University Press, 1986).
8. The quotation is from Liberman's *Take Off Your Glasses and See: A Mind/Body Approach to Expanding Your Eyesight and Insight* (NY: Three Rivers Press, 1995), p. 58.
9. William A. Tiller, *Science and Human Transformation: Subtle Energies, Intentionality, and Consciousness* (Walnut Creek, CA: Pavior Publishing, 1997). Tiller's comprehensive work is a must-read for foundational information and a clear introduction to the quantum world of energy and consciousness.
10. Works by the authors listed can all be found in the bibliography. Most of the authors' original books are now available in the most recent editions. These authors and many others provided us with a wealth of information, and direction to our own New Worlds. A note including everyone would be as long as the bibliographic section itself (smile).
11. Both *What The Bleep* and *The Secret* have websites you can visit to learn more and purchase videos. Go to http://www.whatthebleep.com/ and http://thesecret.tv/. Another good video source is Amit Goswami's 2009 film *The Quantum Activist*. Goswami has long been an activist and scientific pioneer. For more information on his work, go to http://www.amitgoswami.org/.
12. Fred Alan Wolf, *Mind Into Matter: A New Alchemy of Science and Spirit* (Portsmouth, NH: Moment Point Press, 2001), p. 57.
13. Tiller, *Science and Human Transformation*, p. xv.

14. Masaru Emoto, *The Hidden Messages in Water,* translated by David A. Thayne (NY: Atria Books, 2004), p. 39.

15. See especially Rupert Sheldrake, *The Presence of the Past: Morphic Resonance and the Habits of Nature* (Rochester, VT: Park Street Press, 1995) and *Morphic Resonance: The Nature of Formative Causation* (Rochester, VT: Park Street Press, 2009). Sheldrake provides fuller definitions of these working terms in the glossary section of his website, http://www.sheldrake.org/research/glossary/. I provide three of the definitions from this site below:

    Morphic unit: "A unit of form or organization, such as an atom, molecule, crystal, cell, plant, animal, pattern of instinctive behavior, social group, element of culture, ecosystem, planet, planetary system or galaxy. Morphic units are organized in nested hierarchies of units within units: a crystal, for example, contains molecules, which contain atoms, which contain electrons and nuclei, which contain nuclear particles, which contain quarks" (p. 4).

    Morphic field: "A field within and around a morphic unit which organizes its characteristic structure and pattern of activity. Morphic fields underlie the form and behavior of morphic units at all levels of complexity. The term morphic field includes morphogenetic, behavioral, social, cultural and mental fields. Morphic fields are shaped and stabilized by morphic resonance from previous similar morphic units, which were under the influence of fields of the same kind. They consequently contain a kind of cumulative memory and tend to become increasingly habitual" (p. 4).

    Morphic resonance: "The influence of previous structures of activity on subsequent similar structures of activity organized by morphic fields. Through morphic resonance, formative causal influences pass through or across both space and time " (p. 4).

16. A review of Watson and Blair's work can be found on Wikipedia, http://en.wikipedia.org/wiki/Hundreth_monkey_effect/.

17. See especially Sheldrake's *Presence of the Past* where, in his own words, he explores "the wider nature of morphic fields in their behavioral, social, and cultural contexts, and their implications

for the understanding of animal and human memory" (*Morphic Resonance,* p. xxii).

18. From Alexander Pope's "Essay on Criticism," l. 298, in *The Poems of Alexander Pope,* ed. John Butt (New Haven, CN: Yale University Press, 1963), p. 153.
19. Wayne Dyer, *You'll See It When You Believe It* (London: Arrow Books, 2005).
20. Some of my favorites in this huge topic area include Tiller, *Science and Human Transformation*; Fred Alan Wolf, *Taking The Quantum Leap: The New Physics for Nonscientists* (NY: Harper & Row Publishers, 1989); Michael Talbot, The Holographic Universe (NY: Harper Perennial, 20122); Amit Goswami's video *The Quantum Activist* (2009), and his *The Self-Aware Universe: How Consciousness Creates The Material World* (NY: Jeremy P. Tarcher/Putnam, 1995); Robert Lanza, *Biocentrism:How Life and Consciousness are the Keys to Understanding the True Nature of the Universe* (Dallas, TX: BenBella Books, 2009); and for an entertaining and informative overview, the movie *What The Bleep Do We Know!?* (2004).
21. Lynne McTaggart, *The Intention Experiment: Using Your Thoughts To Change Your Life And The World* (NY: Free Press, 2007), p. xviii.
22. Gregg Braden, *The Spontaneous Healing of Belief: Shattering the Paradigm of False Limits* (Carlsbad, CA: Hay House, Inc. 2008), p. 68.
23. See Napoleon Hill, *Think and Grow Rich* (Lexington, KY: SoHo Books, 2012), and *The Law of Success* (NY: Jeremy P. Tarcher/ Penguin, 2008).
24. John Veltheim uses this term throughout his courses on consciousness and quantum healing. These courses are offered in a series under the title, *Finding Health: Mapping the Healing Process.* For more information, go to http://www.bodytalksystem.com/.
25. See especially Bruce Lipton, *The Biology of Belief: Unleashing the Power of Consciousness, Matter, and Miracles* (Santa Rosa, CA: Mountain of Love/Elite Books, 2005) and Dawson Church, *The Genie in Your Genes: Epigenetic Medicine and the New Biology of Intention* (Santa Rosa CA: Energy Psychology Press, 2009). The power of intention or belief to affect health is a foundation concept of alternative health and much older "power of mind" practices.

26. See especially Fred Gallo, *Energy Psychology: Explorations at the Interface of Energy, Cognition, Behavior, and Health* (Boca Raton, FL: CRC Press, 1999) and David Feinstein, Donna Eden, and Gary Craig, *The Promise of Energy Psychology: Revolutionary Tools for Dramatic Personal Change* (NY: Jeremy P. Tarcher/Penguin, 2005). You can also visit Gary Craig's website http://www.emofree.com/.

27. For EFT instruction you can watch an EFT video at http://www.eft.mercola.com/ and get free materials at http://www.eftfree.net/.

28. To explore PSYCH-K, go to http://www.psych-k.com/. To learn more about Theta Healing, see founder Vianna Stibal's *Theta Healing* (Idaho Falls, ID: Rolling Thunder Publishing, 2008) or go to http://www.thetahealing.com/. For BodyTalk, see founder John Veltheim's books, *The BodyTalk System: The Missing Link to Optimum Health* (Sarasota, FL: PaRama, Inc., 1999) and *The Science and Philosophy of BodyTalk: Healthcare Designed for Your Body* (Sarasota, FL: PaRama LLC, 2013) or go to http://www.bodytalksystem.com/. For Resonance Repatterning go to http://resonancerepatterning.net/ and see also founder Chloe Faith Wordsworth's book, *Quantum Change Made Easy: Breakthroughs in Personal Transformation, Self-healing and Achieving the Best of Who You Are* (Scottsdale, AZ: Resonance Publishing, 2007).

Part Two: Portals to Power

1. See John Diamond, *Your Body Doesn't Lie* (NY: Warner Books, 1979). Dr. George Goodheart introduced applied kinesiology after World War II, and practiced and wrote about it throughout a long life and career. For an overview of his work, see http://en.wikipedia.org/wiki/George_Goodheart/.

2. Masaru Emoto, *The Hidden Messages in Water* (NY: Atria Books, 2004).

3. See my article, "Lycidas: Milton's Doric Lay," in *Notes & Queries*, New Series, Vol. 28, No. 3 (June 1981), 202–205.

4. For a description of how to AK test, you can go to Donna Eden's *Energy Medicine*, p. 77, or watch her YouTube video from 2007

demonstrating the basic AK or "energy testing" method, as she calls it, Energy Healing One—03- Energy testing Part 1, uploaded October 25, 2007. Also visit http://etouchforhealth.com/ for a good look at research on the validity of AK. To learn methods for a self-AK test, see my website, http://www.humanrenaissance.com/.

5. Echo Garrett, "Mind Over Matter," in *New You: The Future of Beauty and Anti-Aging,* Summer 2013, pp. 66–9.
6. Tatiana Boncompagni, "Changing Direction," in *New You*, op. cit., p.120.
7. Many thanks to Terri Dodge, Ph.D., one of the most talented distance healers I know. You can visit her website at http://www.followthenaturalpath.com/. For more information on the NeuroModulation Technique, go to http://www.nmt.md/.
8. Thanks to Janet Galipo, D.O.M., senior BodyTalk practitioner and instructor, for this great analogy. You can visit her website at http://www.janetgalipo.com/.
9. Candace Pert, *Molecules of Emotion: The Science Behind Mind-Body Medicine* (NY: Scribner, 2003).
10. Ibid., p.285.
11. Norman Cousins, *Anatomy Of An Illness: As Perceived By The Patient* (NY: W.W. Norton & Company, 1979). The Introduction by Rene Dubos provides an extremely insightful re-view of "special cases" and alternative health in history.
12. Karla McLaren, *The Language of Emotions: What Your Feelings Are Trying to Tell You,* (Boulder, CO: Sounds True, Inc., 2012), p.26.
13. Gratitude to Dr. Andrea Rentea of The Paulina Medical Clinic in Chicago, who said these wise words—and many more.
14. Many thanks to Dr. Bruno Cortis of Chicago, and again to Dr. Andrea Rentea for her steadfast care and for the many wonderful referrals, including this one.
15. For good basic definitions of bodywork modalities, go to http://www.massagetherapy.com and scroll down the extensive glossary. For Feldenkrais, go to http://www.feldenkrais.com. For CranioSacral therapy, go to the Upledger Institute site at http://www.upledger.com. For Naprapathy, go to the Americam

Naprapathic Association site at http://www.naprapathy.org.

16. For resources and information on the heart-brain, see especially the Heartmath site at http://www.heartmath.com/. Almost all alternative healing modalities and techniques emphasize the importance of the heart-brain in total body/mind wellness.

17. See David Feinstein, et al., *The Promise of Energy Psychology.* Gary Craig is now retired; see his site http://www.emofree.com/. Good resources for learning basic EFT include a video at http://www.eft.mercola.com/ and free materials at http://www.eftfree.net/.

18. There are now many popular books, videos, and other resource materials on the complex functions of our brain. For an interesting review of the mind/brain, see Rick Hanson's *Buddha's Brain: The Practical Neuroscience of Happiness, Love, and Wisdom* (Oakland, CA: New Harbinger Publications, Inc., 2009).

19. The term "workshop" is used in the series of courses called *MindScape,* taught within the BodyTalk System, http://www.bodytalksystem.com/.

20. Reprinted with permission. Many thanks to Jenna Schulman!

21. I first learned the term "treasure map" from Shakti Gawain's, *Creative Visualization: Use the Power of Your Imagination to Create What You Want in Your Life* (Novato, CA: Nataraj Publishing, 2002), pp.147-151.

22. See EFT video at http://www.eft.mercola.com/ and free materials at http://www.eftfree.net/.

23. Donna Eden and David Feinstein, *Energy Medicine* (NY: Tarcher/Putnam, 2008).

24. Go to http://www.innersource.net/.

25. Diane Stein, *Essential Reiki: A Complete Guide to an Ancient Healing Art* (Freedom, CA: The Crossing Press, Inc., 1995).

26. Many thanks to Susan I. Schiedel of Miami Beach, Certified BodyTalk practitioner and Licensed Massage Therapist, for her help and support.

27. Gratitude to Michael Blawat, formerly of Michael's Antique Jewelers in Amherst, NY.

28. Juliu Horvath, from the video "Awaken the Flow Within—Inspirational Journey with Juliu Horvath," produced April 1, 2013, by ElephantTribe, http://www.elephanttribe.org/. Juliu is the creator of the Gyrotonic® Expansion Method, which you can learn about at http://www.gyrotonic.com/.

29. See especially Joseph Campbell, *The Hero With a Thousand Faces* (Novato, CA: New World Library, 2008).

30. I found provocative research in Frank Joseph's *Atlantis in Wisconsin: New Revelations about the Lost Sunken City* (Lakeville, MN: Galde Press, 2011), and in his book *The Lost Pyramids of Rock Lake: Wisconsin's Sunken Civilization* (Lakeville, MN: Galde Press, 2009). These books sent me on discovery trips to Wisconsin and other Midwestern ancient sites where artifacts prove a connection to ancient civilizations of Mexico.

31. Melody, *Love Is in the Earth: A Kaleidoscope of Crystals* (Wheat Ridge, CO: Earth-Love Publishing House, 17th printing, 2011).

PART THREE: CHALLENGES TO POWER

1. Susan Jeffers, *Feel the Fear and Do It Anyway* (NY: Ballantine Books, 2007), p. 38.
2. Liberman, *Take Off Your Glasses*, p. 59.
3. Ibid., p. 71.
4. Jeffers, *Feel the Fear*, p. 14.
5. See Erving Goffman's *Frame Analysis: An Essay on the Organization of Experience* (Boston: Northeastern University Press, 1986).
6. One of my favorite discussions of the essay as exploration is Bill Covino's *The Art of Wondering: A Revisionist Return to the History of Rhetoric* (Portsmouth, NH: Boynton/Cook Publishers, 1988).
7. A. Bartlett Giamatti, *Take Time for Paradise: Americans and Their Games* (NY: Summit Books, 1989), p. 40.
8. Although many books and other materials address this topic, for an interesting exploration, see Fred Alan Wolf, *The Yoga of Time Travel:*

How The Mind Can Defeat Time (Wheaton, IL: Quest Books, 2004).

9. Jose Arguelles, *Time and the Technosphere: The Law of Time in Human Affairs* (Rochester, VT: Bear and Company, 2002), p. 4.

10. Gregg Braden, *Fractal Time: The Secret of 2012 and a New World Age* (NY: Hay House, 2009).

11. From Deepak Chopra's *Perfect Health: The Complete Mind/Body Guide* (NY: Harmony Books, 1990), p. 171.

12. See Deepak Chopra and David Simon, *Grow Younger, Live Longer: 10 Steps to Reverse Aging,* (NY: Harmony Books, 2001). The term is used throughout the book, beginning on p. 27.

13. Marshall McLuhan, *Understanding Media* (London: Routledge Classics, 2001), p. 26.

14. Gail Fairhurst and Robert Sarr, *The Art of Framing: Managing the Language of Leadership* (San Francisco: Jossey-Bass Publishers, 1996), pp. xi-xii.

15. Marshall McLuhan, Preface to *The Mechanical Bride*, in *Essential McLuhan*, ed. Eric McLuhan and Frank Zingrone (NY: Basic Books, 1995), p. 21.

16. For a description of how to AK test, you can go to Donna Eden's *Energy Medicine,* p. 77, or watch her YouTube video from 2007 demonstrating the basic AK or energy testing method, as she calls it. See Energy Healing One—03- Energy testing Part 1, uploaded October 25, 2007. Also visit http://etouchforhealth.com/ for a good look at research on the validity of AK.

17. "Chains," stanza 1, lines 1-3. The song was written by Gerry Goffin and Carole King, and had been recorded in 1962 by a group called The Cookies. The Beatles recorded the song on their *Please Please Me* album in 1963, with great success. For the history and full lyrics, go to http://www.beatlesbible.com/song/chains/.

18. Cindy Dale, *The Subtle Body: An Encyclopedia of Your Energetic Anatomy* (Boulder, CO: Sounds True, Inc. 2009), p. 3.

19. Paula Abdul, "Straight Up," 1988, refrain, line 4. All the lyrics for this song can be found at http://metrolyrics.com/printlyric/straight-up-lyrics-paula-abdul.html/.

20. From the author's 2010 interview with W. David Kubiak, see http://www.nancho.net/advisors/mander.html/.

Part Four: Realizing Our Renaissance

1. Campbell, *Hero With A Thousand Faces* (2008).
2. Gerald Pollack, *The Fourth Phase of Water: Beyond Solid, Liquid, And Vapor* (Seattle, WA: Ebner & Sons Publishing, 2013), p. 338.
3. Ibid., p. 339.
4. For information on the classic meditation technique of Transcendental Meditation, go to http://www.tm.org/. Many resources give basic meditation instructions. You can visit sites such as http://www.ananda.org/ or http://www.life.gaiam.com for examples. You may also want to sample some of the many guided mediation CDs.

BIBLIOGRAPHY

Amen, Daniel G. *Healing the Hardware of the Soul.* New York: The Free Press, 2002.

American Society of Dowsers. *Basic Dowsing School Materials.* Danville, VT: American Society of Dowsers, n.d.

Arguelles, Jose. *Time and the Technosphere: The Law of Time in Human Affairs.* Rochester, VT: Bear and Company, 2002.

Ashcroft-Nowicki, Dolores and J.H. Brennan. *Magical Use of Thoughtforms: A Proven System of Mental and Spiritual Empowerment.* St. Paul, MN: Llewellyn Publications, 2002.

Axelrod, Alan. *Elizabeth I CEO: Strategic Lessons from the Leader Who Built an Empire.* New York: Prentice Hall Press, 2000.

Bach, Richard. *Messiah's Handbook: Reminders for the Advanced Soul.* Faber, VA: Rainbow Ridge Books, 2004.

Bailey, Alice. *Ponder on This.* 9th ed. New York: Lucis Press, 1996.

Balch, Phyllis A. *Prescription for Nutritional Healing.* NY: Penguin Group (USA) Inc., 2010.

Bartlett, Richard. *Matrix Energetics: A Hands-on Guide to Subtle Energy and Radical Change.* New York: Atria Books, 2007.

Beaulieu, John. *Human Tuning: Sound Healing with Tuning Forks.* High Falls: BioSonic Enterprises, 2010.

Becker, Robert O. and Gary Selden. *The Body Electric: Electromagnetism and the Foundation of Life.* NY: William Morrow, 1985.

Beinfield, Harriet and Efrem Korngold. *Between Heaven and Earth: A Guide to Chinese Medicine.* New York: Ballantine Books, 1991.

Bender, Sheila Sidney and Mary T. Sise. *The Energy of Belief.* Santa Rosa, CA: Energy Psychology Press, 2008.

Borgault, Luc. *American Indian Secrets of Crystal Healing.* London: Quantum, 1997.

Braden, Gregg. *The Spontaneous Healing of Belief: Shattering the Paradigm of False Limits.* Carlsbad, CA: Hay House Inc. 2008.

———. *Fractal Time: The Secret of 2012 and a New World Age.* New York: Hay House Inc. 2009.

———. *The Divine Matrix: Bridging Time, Space, Miracles, and Belief.* New York: Hay House Inc. 2010.

Bragg, Paul C. *Toxicless Diet: Body Purification and Healing System.* Santa Barbara, CA: Health Science, 1992.

Brennan, Barbara Ann. *Hands of Light: A Guide to Healing through the Human Energy Field.* New York: Bantam Books, 1987.

Brotton, Jerry. *The Renaissance: A Very Short Introduction.* New York: Oxford University Press, 2006.

Bruce, Robert and Brian Mercer. *Mastering Astral Projection: 90-Day Guide to Out-of-Body Experience.* St. Paul, MN: Llewellyn Publications, 2005.

Burke, Kenneth. *On Symbols and Society.* Edited by Joseph R. Gusfield. Chicago: University of Chicago Press, 1989.

Campbell, Joseph. *The Hero With A Thousand Faces.* Novato, CA: New World Library, 2008.

Cerney, J.V. *Acupuncture without Needles.* New York: Prentice Hall Press, 1999.

Chopra, Deepak. *Perfect Health: The Complete Mind/Body Guide.* New York: Harmony Books, 1990.

Chopra, Deepak and David Simon. *Grow Younger, Live Longer: 10 Steps to Reverse Aging.* New York: Harmony Books, 2001.

Church, Dawson. *The Genie in Your Genes: Epigenetic Medicine and the New Biology of Intention.* Santa Rosa, CA: Energy Psychology Press, 2009.

Clow, Barbara Hand. *Catastrophobia: The Truth behind Earth Changes.* Rochester,VT: Bear and Company, 2001.

———. The Mayan Code: *Time Acceleration and Awakening the World Mind.* Rochester, VT: Bear and Company, 2007.

Co, Stephen and Eric B. Robins. *Your Hands Can Heal You: Pranic Healing*

Energy Remedies to Boost Vitality and Speed Recovery from Common Health Problems. New York: Free Press, 2002.

Cousins, Norman. Anatomy *Of An Illness: As Perceived By The Patient.* NY: W.W. Norton & Company, 1979.

Covino, William A. *The Art of Wondering: A Revisionist Return to the History of Rhetoric.* Portsmouth, NH: Boynton/Cook Publishers, 1988.

Cowan, Thomas S. with Sally Fallon and Jaimen McMillan. *The Fourfold Path to Healing.* Washington, DC: NewTrends Publishing, Inc. 2004.

Csikszentmihalyi, Mihaly. *Flow: The Psychology of Optimal Experience.* New York: Harper Perennial, 1991.

Dale, Cyndi. *The Subtle Body: An Encyclopedia of Your Energetic Anatomy.* Boulder, CO: Sounds True Inc. 2009.

Diamond, John. *Your Body Doesn't Lie.* New York: Warner Books, 1979.

DuQuette, Lon Milo. *Enochian Vision Magick: An Introduction and Practical Guide to the Magick of D. John Dee and Edward Kelly.* San Francisco: Red Wheel/Weiser LLC, 2008.

Dyer, Wayne W. *The Power of Intention: Learning to Co-Create Your World Your Way.* Carlsbad, CA: Hay House Inc., 2004.

———. *You'll See It When You Believe It.* London: Arrow Books, 2005.

———. *Wishes Fulfilled: Mastering the Art of Manifesting.* New Delhi: Hay House, 2012.

Eden, Donna and David Feinstein. *Energy Medicine.* New York: Tarcher/Putnam, 1999, 2008.

Eisenstein, Charles. *Sacred Economics: Money, Gift, and Society in the Age of Transition.* Berkeley: Evolver Editions, 2011.

Emoto, Masaru. Trans. David A. Thayne. *The Hidden Messages in Water.* New York: Atria Books, 2004.

Fairhurst, Gail T. and Robert A. Sarr. *The Art of Framing: Managing the Language of Leadership.* San Francisco: Jossey-Bass Publishers, 1996.

Faure-Alderson, Martine. *Total Reflexology: The Reflex Points for Physical, Emotional, and Psychological Healing.* Rochester, VT: Healing Arts Press, 2008.

Feinstein, David, Donna Eden, and Gary Craig. *The Promise Of Energy*

Psychology: Revolutionary Tools for Dramatic Personal Change. New York: Jeremy P. Tarcher/Penguin, 2005.

Feldenkrais, Moshe. *Awareness through Movement.* New York: Harper Collins Publishers, 1990.

———. *Body Awareness As Healing Therapy: The Case of Nora.* Berkeley: Frog Ltd., 1993.

Fehmi, Les and Jim Robbins. *The Open-Focus Brain: Harnessing the Power of Attention to Heal Mind and Body.* Boston: Trumpeter, 2007.

Fish, Stanley. *Self-Consuming Artifacts: The Experience of Seventeenth-Century Literature.* Berkeley: University of California Press, 1972.

Forem, Jack and Steve Shimer. *Healing with Pressure Point Therapy.* Paramus, NJ: Prentice Hall, 1999.

Friedlander, John and Gloria Hemsher. *Basic Psychic Development: A User's Guide to Auras, Chakras, and Clairvoyance.* York Beach, ME: Weiser Books, 1999.

Fuchs, Nan Kathryn. *Color Me Healthy.* Norcross, GA: Soundview Communication Inc., 2010.

Gallo, Fred P. *Energy Psychology: Explorations at the Interface of Energy, Cognition, Behavior, and Health.* Boca Raton, FL: CRC Press, 1999.

Gawain, Shakti. *Creative Visualization: Use the Power of Your Imagination to Create What You Want in Your Life.* Novato, CA: Nataraj Publishing, 2002.

Gerber, Richard. *Vibrational Medicine for the 21st Century.* New York: HaperCollins, 2000.

Giamatti, A. Bartlett. *The Earthly Paradise and the Renaissance Epic.* New York: W.W. Norton and Company, 1966.

———. *Exile and Change in Renaissance Literature.* New Haven: Yale University Press, 1984.

———. *Take Time for Paradise: Americans and Their Games.* New York: Summit Books, 1989.

Goffman, Erving. *Frame Analysis: An Essay on the Organization of Experience.* Boston: Northeastern University Press, 1986.

Goldman, Jonathan. *Healing Sounds: The Power of Harmonics.* Rochester, VT: Healing Arts Press, 2002.

Goodman, Felicitas D. and Nana Nauwald. *Ecstatic Trance: A Workbook.* Havelte/Holland: Binkey Kok Publications, 2003.

Gordon, Richard. *Quantum Touch 2.0: The New Human.* Berkeley: North Atlantic Books, 2013.

Gore, Belinda. *Ecstatic Body Postures: An Alternate Reality Workbook.* Rochester, VT: Bear and Company, 1995.

Goswami, Amit. *The Self-Aware Universe: How Consciousness Creates The Material World.* NY: Jeremy Tarcher/Putnam, 1995.

———. *The Visionary Window: A Quantum Physicist's Guide to Enlightenment.* Wheaton, IL: Quest Books, 2000.

———. *The Quantum Doctor.* Charlottesville, VA: Hampton Roads Publishing Co. Inc., 2004.

Goulston, Mark, and Philip Goldberg. *Get Out of Your Own Way: Overcoming Self-defeating Behavior.* New York: Penguin Group, 1996.

Goulston, Mark. *Just Listen: Discover the Secret to Getting through to Absolutely Anyone.* New York: American Management Association, 2010.

Greene, Brian. *The Hidden Reality: Parallel Universes and the Deep Laws of the Cosmos.* New York: Alfred A. Knopf, 2011.

Grey, Alex with Ken Wilber and Carlo McCormick. *Sacred Mirrors: The Visionary Art of Alex Grey.* Rochester, VT: Inner Traditions International, 1990.

Hall, Judy. *The Crystal Bible: A Definitive Guide to Crystals.* Cincinnati, OH: Walking Stick Press, 2003.

Hancock, Graham. *Finger Prints of the Gods: The Evidence of Earth's Lost Civilization.* New York: Three Rivers Press, 1995.

Hanh, Tich Nat. *Breathe! You Are Alive: Sutra on the Full Awareness of Breathing.* Berkeley: Parallax Press, 1996.

———. *The Art of Power.* New York: Harper Collins, 2007.

Hanson, Rick, with Richard Mendius. *Buddha's Brain: the practical neuroscience of happiness, love & wisdom.* Oakland, CA: New Harbinger Publications, Inc. 2009.

Hay, Louise and Mona Lisa Schulz. *All Is Well: Heal Your Body with Medicine, Affirmations, and Intuition.* N.p.:Hay House, 2013.

Hiestand, Denie and Shellie Hiestand. *Electrical Nutrition.* New York: Avery, 2001.

Hill, Napoleon. *The Law of Success.* New York: Jeremy P. Tarcher/Penguin, 2008.

———. *Think and Grow Rich.* Lexington, KY: SoHo Books, 2010.

Houston, Jean. *The Wizard of Us: Transformational Lessons from Oz.* New York: Atria Books, 2012.

Jacka, Judith. *The Vivaxis Connection: Healing through Earth Energies.* Charlottesville, VA: Hampton Roads Publishing Company Inc., 2000.

Jeffers, Susan. *Feel the Fear and Do It Anyway.* New York: Ballantine Books, 2007.

Jenkins, John Major. *Maya Cosmogenesis 2012: The True Meaning of the Maya Calendar End-Date.* Rochester, VT: Bear and Company, 1998.

———. *Galactic Alignment: The Transformation of Consciousness according to Mayan, Egyptian, and Vedic Traditions.* Rochester, VT: Bear and Company, 2002.

Johnson, Mark. *The Body in the Mind: The Bodily Basis of Meaning, Imagination, and Reason.* Chicago: University of Chicago Press, 1987.

Joseph, Frank. *The Lost Pyramids of Rock Lake: Wisconsin's Sunken Civilization.* Lakeville, MN: Galde Press, 2009.

———. *Atlantis in Wisconsin: New Revelations about Lost Sunken City.* Lakeville, MN: Galde Press, 2011.

Kaelin, Angela. *All Natural Dental Remedies.* N.p. Winter Tempest Books, 2012.

Karim, Ibrahim. *Back to a Future for Mankind: BioGeometry.* N.p.: BioGeometry Consulting Ltd., 2010.

Kaptchuk, Ted J. *The Web That Has No Weaver: Understanding Chinese Medicine.* New York: McGraw-Hill, 2000.

Kelder, Peter. *The Eye of Revelation.* Bayside, CA: Borderland Sciences Research Foundation, 1975.

Kloss, Jethro. *Back to Eden: A Human Interest Story of Health and Restoration to be Found in Herb, Root, and Bark.* Twin Lakes, WI: Lotus Press, 2002.

Knight, Christopher and Robert Lomas. *Uriel's Machine: Uncovering the*

Secrets of Stonehenge, Noah's flood, and the Dawn of Civilization. Gloucester, MA: Fair Winds Press, 2001.

Koch, Liz. *The Psoas Book.* Felton, CA: Guinea Pig Publications, 1997.

Kunz, Barbara and Kevin. *Reflexology: health at your fingertips.* NewYork: DK Publishing, Inc., 2003.

Lanza, Robert. *Biocentrism: How Life and Consciousness Are the Keys to Understanding the True Nature of the Universe.* Dallas: Benbella Books Inc., 2009.

Levine, Peter A. with Ann Frederick. *Waking the Tiger: Healing Trauma.* Berkeley: North Atlantic Books, 1997.

Liberman, Jacob. *Light: Medicine of the Future.* Rochester, VT: Bear and Company, 1991.

———. *Take Off Your Glasses and See: A Mind/Body Approach to Expanding Your Eyesight and Insight.* New York: Three Rivers Press, 1995.

Lilly, Sue and Simon Lilly. *Healing with Crystals and Chakra Energies.* New York: Barnes and Noble Books, 2005.

Linn, Denise. *Sacred Space: Clearing and Enhancing the Energy of Your Home.* New York: Ballantine Books, 1995.

Lipton, Bruce. *The Biology of Belief: Unleashing the Power of Consciousness, Matter, and Miracles.* Santa Rosa, CA: Mountain of Love/Elite Books, 2005.

Schwaller de Lubicz, R.A. *The Temple in Man: Sacred Architecture and the Perfect Man.* Translated by Robert Lawlor and Deborah Lawlor. Rochester, VT: Inner Traditions International, 1981.

Mander, Jerry. *Four Arguments for the Elimination of Television.* New York: Harper Collins Publishers, 1978; reprinted Perennial, 2002.

Marciniak, Barbara. *Family of Light.* Rochester, VT: Bear and Company, 1999.

———. *Path of Empowerment.* Maui, HI: Inner Ocean Publishing, 2004.

McLaren, Karla. *The Language of Emotions: What Your Feelings Are Trying to Tell You.* Boulder, CO: Sounds True Inc., 2010.

McLuhan, Marshall. *Essential McLuhan.* Edited by Eric McLuhan and Frank Zingrone. New York: Basic Books, 1995.

McTaggart, Lynne. *The Field: The Quest for the Secret Force of the Universe.* New York: Harper Collins, 2002.

———. *The Intention Experiment: Using Your Thoughts to Change Your Life and the World.* New York: Free Press, 2007.

Melody. *Love is in the Earth: A Kaleidoscope of Crystals.* Wheat Ridge, CO: Earth-Love Publishing House, Seventeenth Printing, 2004.

Mercier, Patricia. *Chakras: Balance Your Body's Energy for Health and Harmony.* New York: Sterling Publishing Company Inc., 2000.

Michalski, Anthony R. and Robert Schmitz. *The Master Key Workbook.* Wilkes-Barre, PA: Kallisti Publishing, 2004.

Michelet, Jules. *Histoire De France Au Seizieme Siecle: Renaissance.* Paris: Chamerot, Librarie-Editeur, 1855, Kindle edition.

Milton, John. *Complete Poems and Major Prose.* Edited by Merritt Y. Hughes. New York: The Odyssey Press Inc., 1957.

Moritz, Andreas. *Cancer is NOT a Disease! It's a Survival Mechanism.* N.p.: Ener-Chi Wellness Press, 2009.

Murphy, Joseph. *The Power of Your Subconscious Mind.* Radford: Wilder Publications, LLC, 2007.

Myss, Carolyn *Anatomy of the Spirit: The Seven Stages of Power and Healing.* New York: Three Rivers Press, 1996.

———. *Why People Don't Heal and How They Can.* New York: Three Rivers Press, 1997.

———. *Sacred Contracts: Awakening Your Divine Potential.* New York: Harmony Books, 2001.

———. *Defy Gravity; Healing Beyond the Bounds of Reason.* Carlsbad, CA: Hay House Inc., 2009.

Nagel, Ramiel. *Cure Tooth Decay: Heal & Prevent Cavities with Nutrition.* Ashland, OR: Golden Child Publishing, 2012.

Ogden, C.K. and I.A. Richards. *The Meaning of Meaning.* Orlando, FL: Harcourt Brace Jovanovich Inc., 1989.

Osho. *Body Mind Balancing: Using Your Mind to Heal Your Body.* New York: St. Martin's Griffin, 2003.

Oswald, Yvonne. *Every Word Has Power: Switch on Your Language and Turn on Your Life*. New York: Atria Books, 2008.

Pearce, Joseph Chilton. *The Biology of Transcendance: A Blueprint of the Human Spirit*. Rochester, VT: Park Street Press, 2004.

Pearman, Roger R. and Sarah C. Albritton. *I'm Not Crazy I'm Just Not You*. Boston: Nicholas Brealey Publishing, 2010.

Pearsall, Paul. *The Heart's Code: Tapping the Wisdom and Power of Our Heart Energy*. New York: Broadway Books, 1999.

Peirce, Penney. *Frequency: The Power of Personal Vibration*. New York: Atria Books, 2009.

Pert, Candace. *Molecules of Emotion: The Science behind Mind-Body Medicine*. New York: Scribner, 2003.

Peterson, Natasha. *Sacred Sites: A Traveler's Guide to North America's Most Powerful, Mystical Landmarks*. Chicago: Contemporary Books Inc., 1988.

Pinchbeck, Daniel. *2012: The Return of Quetzalcoatl*. New York: Jeremy Tarcher/Penguin, 2006.

Pinchbeck, Daniel and Ken Jordan, eds. *Toward 2012: Perspectives on the Next Age*. New York: Jeremy P. Tarcher/Penguin, 2008.

Pollack, Gerald H. *The Fourth Phase of Water: Beyond Solid, Liquid, And Vapor*. Seattle, WA: Ebner & Sons Publishers, 2013.

Ponder, Catherine. *The Dynamic Laws of Prosperity*. Marina Del Rey: DeVorss and Company, 1997.

Pope, Alexander. *The Poems of Alexander Pope*. Edited by John Butt. New Haven: Yale University Press, 1963.

The Quantum Activist. Dir. Ri Stewart and Renee Slade. Intention Media, 2009. DVD.

Romaner, Kim Marcille. *The Science of Making Things Happen*. Novato, CA: New World Library, 2010.

Rosenblum, Bruce and Fred Kuttner. *Quantum Enigma: Physics Encounters Consciousness*. Oxford: Oxford University Press, 2011.

Samanta-Laughton, Manjir. *Punk Science: Inside The Mind Of God*. Winchester, UK: O Books, 2006.

Sarno, John E. *The Divided Mind: The Epidemic of Mindbody Disorders*. New York: Harper Collins, 2007.

Schulz, Mona Lisa. *Awakening Intuition: Using Your Mind-Body Network for Insight and Healing.* New York: Three Rivers Press, 1998.

Seale, Alan. *The Manifestation Wheel: A Practical Process for Creating Miracles.* San Francisco: RedWheel/Weiser LLC, 2008.

The Secret. Dir. Drew Heriot. Prime Time Productions, 2006. DVD.

Senzon, Sandra. *Reversing Gum Disease Naturally: A Holistic Home Care Program.* Hoboken, NJ: John Wiley & Sons, Inc., 2003.

Shafarman, Steven. *Awareness Heals: The Feldenkrais Method for Dynamic Health.* Reading, MA: Perseus Books, 1997.

Shapiro, Deb. *Your Body Speaks Your Mind: Decoding the Emotional, Psychological, and Spiritual Messages That Underlie Illness.* Boulder, CO: Sounds True Inc., 2006.

Shinskey, Clare McCord. "Lycidas: Milton's Doric Lay." *Notes and Queries.* New Series. Vol. 28 No. 3. June 1981, pp. 202–205.

Sheldrake, Rupert. *The Presence of the Past: Morphic Resonance and the Habits of Nature.* Rochester, VT: Park Street Press, 1995.

———. *Seven Experiments That Could Change the World: A Do-It-Yourself Guide to Revolutionary Science.* Rochester, VT: Park Street Press, 2002.

———. *Morphic Resonance: The Nature of Formative Causation.* Rochester, VT: Park Street Press, 2009.

———. *Science Set Free: 10 Paths to New Discovery.* New York: Deepak Chopra Books, 2012.

Simmons, Robert. *Stones of the New Consciousness.* Berkeley: North Atlantic Books, 2009.

Simpson, Liz. *The Book of Chakra Healing.* New York: Sterling Publishing Company Inc., 1999.

———. *The Healing Energies of Earth.* Boston: Journey Editions, 2000.

Spencer, Robert. *The Craft of the Warrior.* Berkeley: Frog Ltd., 2006.

Stavish, Mark. *Between the Gates: Lucid Dreaming, Astral Projection, and the Body of Light in Western Esotericism.* San Francisco: Weiser Books, 2008.

———. *The Path of Alchemy: Energetic Healing and the World of Natural Magic.* Woodbury, MN: Llewellyn Publications, 2007.

Stein, Diane. *Essential Reiki: A Complete Guide to an Ancient Healing Art.* Freedom, CA: The Crossing Press Inc., 1995.

Steiner, Rudolph. *How to Know Higher Worlds.* Trans. by Christopher Bamford and Sabine Seiler. N.p.: Anthroposophic Press, 1994.

Stibal, Vianna. *Theta Healing.* Idaho Falls, ID: Rolling Thunder Publishing, 2008.

Sylver, Nenah. *The Rife Handbook of Frequency Therapy with a Holistic Health Primer.* Phoenix: Desert Gate Productions LLC, 2009.

Talbot, Michael. *The Holographic Universe.* New York: Harper Perennial, 2011.

Targ, Russell. *Limitless Mind: A Guide to Remote Viewing and Transformation of Consciousness.* Novato, CA: New World Library, 2004.

Thie, John, and Matthew Thie. *Touch for Health: A Practical Guide to Natural Health with Acupressure Touch.* Camarillo, CA: DeVorss Publications, 2005; sixth printing, 2012.

Thie, John. *Touch for Health Reference Portfolio: Acupressure Touch and Massage with Muscle Testing for Postural Balance.* Marina del Rey, CA: Devorss and Company, 2001.

Thomas, Linnie. Edited by Carrie Obry. *The Encyclopedia of Energy Medicine.* Minneapolis: Fairview Press, 2010.

Tiller, William A. *Science and Human Transformation: Subtle Energies, Intentionality, and Consciousness.* Walnut Creek, CA: Pavior Publishing, 1997.

Tolle, Eckhart. *The Power of Now: A Guide to Spiritual Enlightenment.* Novato, CA: New World Library, 1999.

Trumfheller, Susan Bacon. *99 Ways to Use the Pendulum.* California: Discovery Press, 2010.

Trungpa, Chogyam. *Shambahala: The Sacred Path of the Warrior.* Boston: Shambahala Publications Inc., 1988.

Ury, William. *Getting Past No: Negotiating Your Way from Confrontation to Cooperation.* New York: Bantam Books, 1993.

Valentine, Tom and Carole Valentine, with Douglas P. Hetrick. *Applied Kinesiology.* Rochester, VT: Healing Arts Press, 1987.

Veltheim, John. *The BodyTalk System: The Missing Link to Optimum Health.* Sarasota, FL: PaRama Inc., 1999.

———. *The Science and Philosophy of BodyTalk: Healthcare Designed by Your Body*. Sarasota, FL: PaRama LLC, 2013.

Walker, D.P. *Spiritual and Demonic Magic from Ficino to Campanella.* Notre Dame: University of Notre Dame Press, 1958.

Wattles, Wallace D. *The Wisdom of Wallace D. Wattles, including the Science of Getting Rich, the Science of Being Great, and the Science of Being Well.* N.p.: BN Publishing, 2006.

Weinstein, Marion. *Positive Magic: Occult Self-Help.* New York: Earth Magic Productions, 1994.

Weir, Alison. *The Life of Elizabeth I.* New York: Ballantine Books, 2008.

What the Bleep Do We Know!? Dir. William Arntz, Betsy Chasse, and Mark Vicente. Roadside Attractions, 2004. DVD.

Wilcock, David. *The Source Field Investigations.* New York: Dutton, 2011.

Wolf, Fred Alan. *Taking the Quantum Leap: The New Physics for Non-scientists.* NY: Harper & Row Publishers, 1989.

———. *Mind into Matter: A New Alchemy of Science and Spirit.* Portsmouth, NH: Moment Point Press, 2001.

———. *The Yoga of Time Travel: How the Mind Can Defeat Time.* Wheaton, IL: Quest Books, 2004.

———. *Dr. Quantum's Little Book of Big Ideas: Where Science Meets Spirit.* Needham, MA: Moment Point Press, 2005.

Wolf, Silver Raven. *Mindlight: Secrets of Energy, Magick, and Manifestation.* Woodbury, MN: Llewellyn Publications, 2006.

Woods, Walt. *Letter to Robin: A Mini-Course in Pendulum Dowsing.* 10th Revision. St. Johnsbury, VT: The American Society of Dowsers, 2001.

Wordsworth, Chloe Faith with Gail Noble Glanville. *Quantum Change Made Easy: Breakthroughs in Personal Transformation, Self-healing and Achieving the Best of Who You Are.* Scottsdale, AZ: Resonance Publishing, 2007.

Zukav, Gary. *The Seat of the Soul.* New York: Fireside, 1989.

Made in the USA
Middletown, DE
08 February 2015